A Private Woman in Public Spaces

AFRICAN AMERICAN
RELIGIOUS THOUGHT AND LIFE

This series provides opportunity for African American scholars from a wide variety of fields in religion to develop their insights into religious discourse on issues that affect African American intellectual, social, cultural, and community life. The series focuses on topics, figures, problems, and cultural expressions in the study of African American religion that are often neglected by publishing programs centered on African American theology. The AARTL program of publications will bridge theological reflection on African American religious experience and the critical, methodological interests of African American religious studies.

SERIES EDITORS

ANTHONY B. PINN, Macalester College, St. Paul, Minnesota
VICTOR ANDERSON, Vanderbilt University, Nashville, Tennessee

Making the Gospel Plain
edited by Anthony B. Pinn

A Private Woman in Public Spaces
Barbara A. Holmes

A Private Woman in Public Spaces

BARBARA JORDAN'S SPEECHES ON ETHICS, PUBLIC RELIGION, AND LAW

Barbara A. Holmes

TRINITY PRESS INTERNATIONAL
Harrisburg, Pennsylvania

Trinity Press International, P.O. Box 1321, Harrisburg, PA 17105
Trinity Press International is a division of the Morehouse Group.

Cover image: Photograph of Barbara Jordan, courtesy of the Robert James Terry
Library, Barbara Jordan Archives, at Texas Southern University.

Cover design: Trude Brummer

Library of Congress Cataloging-in-Publication Data

Holmes, Barbara Ann, 1943-
    A private woman in public spaces : Barbara Jordan's speeches on ethics, public
religion, and law / Barbara A. Holmes.
        p.   cm.
    Includes bibliographical references and index.
    ISBN 1-56338-302-0 (pbk. : alk. paper)
    1. Jordan, Barbara, 1936 – Political and social views. 2. United States – Politics
and government – 1945-1989. 3. United States – Politics and government – 1989.
4. United States – Moral conditions – 20th century. 5. Pluralism (Social sciences)
– United States. 6. Social values – United States. 7. Speeches, addresses, etc.,
American.   I. Title.

E840.8.J62 H65   2000
328.73′092 – dc21
                                                                99-087363

Printed in the United States of America

00   01   02   03   04   05   06   10   9   8   7   6   5   4   3   2   1

Contents

Part Four
THE VISION

Preface

When the story of the twentieth century is told, it will focus not only on its many heroes and antiheroes — its leaders of revolt, its villains, and victors of wars. There will also be a place for ordinary people like Barbara Jordan, who responded in extraordinary ways to the needs of her generation. Drawing on diverse resources, she engaged the social issues of her time through speeches that integrated her beliefs and values in ethics, religion, and law. Jordan's intent was to translate abstract discussions about the common good into the nitty-gritty work of actually creating a better society. That work included her willingness to risk difficult public discussions about immigration, race, and morality. This short biographical sketch is an important preface to the study of Jordan's speeches. Readers who seek more detailed information about her life are encouraged to read currently available biographies.[1]

Born in Houston, Texas, on February 21, 1936, Barbara Charline was the third daughter of Benjamin and Arlyne Jordan. Her sisters Rose Mary and Bennie, grandparents John Ed and Martha Patten, and Alice Reed Jordan (grandmother Gar) and Charles Jordan completed a tightly knit family unit. Jordan's early years were enriched by family nurturing, close community ties in Houston's Fifth Ward, and a strong affiliation with the Good Hope Missionary Baptist Church. She proved to be a good student and skilled orator while in Houston's public schools. Jordan graduated from Phillis Wheatley High School, from Texas Southern University, magna cum laude, and she received her law degree from Boston University Law School.

After law school, she returned to Texas to open a general law practice. Her political career was launched in 1966 when she became the first black female ever elected to public office in Texas and the first black to be elected to the Texas Senate since the end of the nineteenth century.[2] In 1972, Jordan was elected to the U.S. House of Representatives and was assigned to the House Judiciary Committee. Two years later, in 1974 during the impeachment hearings of President Richard Nixon, she delivered a speech on constitutionalism and morality that thrust her into the national limelight.

Many other firsts followed including two keynote addresses before the Democratic National Convention. After being elected to three congressional terms, Jordan retired from public life in 1979 to begin a teaching career at the University of Texas-Austin. She declined to discuss the details of her neuromuscular disease and failing health.[3] Instead, she focused her energy on the issues that mattered the most to her. This book is about those issues: ethics, the common good, law, and religion. On January 17, 1996, the nation mourned Jordan's death. Although her inimitable voice will be missed, her speeches offer an insightful and constructive blueprint for national unity and moral flourishing.

Acknowledgments

Barbara Jordan's inimitable voice and moral goals inspired this book; many people supported my effort. I appreciate the friendship, guidance, and wisdom of Victor Anderson. I also appreciate the research support and assistance of the Barbara Jordan Archives and the professional mentoring of Howard Harrod, Lewis V. Baldwin, Joseph C. Hough, and Susan Ford Wiltshire. I also thank Marcia Y. Riggs, the Rev. Ernestine Cole, and Karen Jenkins for their wisdom and sustaining friendship. During my legal training, Judges Tommy Day Wilcox and Walker P. Johnson, judicial support staff Linda and Sandy, attorney Karl Rice, and moot court partner Rita Coleman honed my skills and my analytical perceptions about the world and the law. My theater friends, Henry, Walter, Grace, and Latonia, encouraged me to explore in that mystical space just beyond human sight. I also have wonderful colleagues and friends at Memphis Theological Seminary.

I am grateful for the grace of God, the empowerment of the Holy Spirit, and the community of Pentecostal believers in Dallas and Miami, who affirmed my call to ministry and teaching. Many journeyed with me during the writing process, offering love, laughter, and support along the way: my creative and talented children, Jason and Marcus; my siblings and life companions, Susan, Eileen, Mildred, and Thomas, and my precious mother, Mildred Holmes. I am also grateful for the lives and wisdom of friends and family absent from the body and present with the Lord: my father, Thomas S. Holmes; grandmother Mildred Schenck; and Vanessa. I also have sister-friends, Catherine, Gwen, Audrey, Ina, Pam, and Anthea, who engage me in late-night phone calls that cheer and inspire me.

When I am researching and writing I sometimes feel as if the Lord, all-night talk radio, and my books are my only companions. This list I have just compiled reminds me that my life is richly blessed, intellectually stimulating, and very full. For all this and more, I give thanks.

Chronology:
Barbara Charline Jordan

1936   Born February 21, in Houston, Texas

1952   Graduation from Phillis Wheatley High School. Winner of
        the National United Ushers Association Oratorical Award

1953   August 15, joined Good Hope Missionary Baptist Church

1956   Graduation from Texas Southern University, magna cum
        laude

        Matriculation at Boston University Law School

        Introduction to the religious perspectives of Howard
        Thurman

1959   Graduation from Boston University Law School

1960   Opens private practice in the Fifth Ward of
        Houston, Texas

1962   Loses first primary race for the Texas Legislature

1964   Loses second primary race for the Texas Legislature

1966   Elected to Texas State Senate

1968   Wins second term to the Texas Senate

1971   Announces candidacy for 18th Congressional District,
        U.S. House of Representatives

1972   Elected to the U.S. House of Representatives; Texas
        Governor for a Day

        Father B. M. Jordan dies

1973   Health declining, diagnosis of multiple sclerosis

1974   July 25, Watergate impeachment hearing speech

1976   First keynote speech at the Democratic National Convention (President Jimmy Carter's nomination)

1979   Retirement from national politics

        Dedication of the Barbara Jordan Archives, Texas Southern University

1982   Appointed to the LBJ Centennial Chair in National Policy, Lyndon Johnson School of Public Affairs, University of Texas-Austin

1987   Testimony against Robert H. Bork's Supreme Court appointment

1988   Seconds nomination of Lloyd Bentsen at the Democratic National Convention

1991   Texas appointment by Governor Ann Richards as Special Counsel for Ethics

1992   Teaching and lecture circuit; second keynote speech at the Democratic National Convention (President Bill Clinton's nomination)

1993   Appointed by President Clinton to Chair of the U.S. Commission on Immigration Reform

1994   Presidential Medal of Freedom

1996   Death on January 17

Part One

The Person

Chapter 1

Introduction

We live in this world in order to contribute to the growth, the development, the spirit and the life of the community of humankind.   — BARBARA JORDAN[1]

Our words stitch us to history and to one another. Every possibility of human transcendence or failure is ultimately filtered through our rhetoric. Words shape, define, and construct fragile legacies for future generations. Ultimately, words last longer than our bodies or our buildings; they reflect an indelible imprint of our times. Barbara Jordan's speeches are such a legacy. Although she was best known for her oratorical skill, her political savvy, and her moral witness to the nation, her speeches encompass more. They provide a glimpse of her comprehensive social vision.

When Jordan emerges as a public figure during the early 1970s, she is an unlikely messenger in the midst of a fluctuating social order. Through her speeches, she responds to the cataclysmic shifts of culture that will forever separate the "Leave It to Beaver" 1950s generation from the social, racial, and class struggles that erupt during the 1960s. This book is the culmination of an interest in Jordan's moral ideals that began when she gave her televised Watergate testimony before the House Judiciary Committee. On that historic occasion, the nation was stunned by her bold presence and centered constitutional arguments. Few missed the irony of the moment. An African American woman embraced and defended a constitution written by slaveholding nation-founders who intended to exclude her from its protections. Jordan acknowledged this historical gap between intent and effect as she steadfastly declared her belief in the precepts that only liminally included her. At the same time, her moral authority created the cognitive dissonance

3

that would reverberate for generations throughout a culturally ambivalent nation.

As the first African American woman to be elected to Congress from the South, she was positioned to speak to a generation on the cusp of change and crisis. These were tumultuous times. Watergate had become a national moral crisis at the same time that the public discontent of ethnic minorities, women, young adults, and radical and conservative factions was at a peak. As groups vied with one another for public attention, the dialogue among them became increasingly caustic.[2] By contrast, Jordan's speeches posit the notion that "the pursuit of community makes reconciliation possible."[3] She also argues that protest and demonstration should not exhaust the potential of the public sphere. This realm, she concludes, is not only the site of debate and contestation, but is also the space where a more relational future can be forged.

To my knowledge, this book offers the first comprehensive analysis of Jordan's written speeches from 1974 to 1995.[4] This period begins with the Watergate years and ends with Jordan's immigration initiatives. Beyond their historical significance, the speeches offer important insights into her moral theories and her model of a flourishing multiethnic society. They also provide insights about a complex and often enigmatic woman whose ideas will be discussed and analyzed for years to come.

On the one hand, Jordan's pragmatic optimism suggests a refreshing approach to intransigent social problems. On the other hand, her commitment to the civic myths of the dominant culture raises questions as to the relevance of her moral theories for marginalized communities. One thing is certain, the speeches create a unique format for the intersection of ethics, public religion, and law. It is at this point of convergence that the potential for a viable national community becomes apparent.

Jordan envisions a national community of mutually obligated sectors of society — a nation and community of nations distinguished by a diverse and responsible citizenry, moral rectitude, shared values, and public discourse. In an era of political radicalism and social rebellion, Jordan's commonsense approach to these issues kindles the interest of liberals, radicals, conservatives, and centrists alike. In effect, she acts as a moral fulcrum for conflicting interest groups and competing versions of moral flourishing. Even those who do not agree with her liberal political stance are compelled to listen to her discussion of public values.

I attribute the universal appeal of Jordan's rhetoric to the broad spectrum of issues engaged in her speeches. She is a staunch proponent of civic duty, constitutionalism, and the liberal agenda of economic success and progress. However, her opposition to the status quo in terms of ethnicity, class, and gender becomes apparent when she critiques the restricted and homogenized view of society that prevailed in North America when she was growing up.[5] All who hear or meet Jordan wonder how a constitutional advocate, centrist politician, and loyal citizen can emerge from a cauldron of racial bias and social inequities. The answers seem to emanate from a family background that nurtures and challenges her to claim her place in the world.

Jordan's concept of a thriving community is drawn in part from her own childhood experiences in Houston's segregated Fifth Ward. In Houston, she develops her moral perspectives and learns of the negative effects on family and friends of white supremacy, gender bias, and class issues. However, she also learns positive and self-sustaining responses to oppression. In fact, experiences that might have engendered an overriding sense of victimization and outrage instead heighten Jordan's awareness of the potential for moral transcendence. This awareness is crucial to her formation.

In general, transcendence assumes that movement can be made toward solutions that are beyond intentional human action. Transcendence also points to connections between finite existence and an overarching and omnipresent infinity that pervades human life. The assumption is that the essence of humanity cannot be totally subsumed in corporeal or intellectual components and that dimensional boundaries are misleading. Social ethicist Howard Harrod explains that "transcendence is made possible through acts of grasping experience in its dimensions of depth, by turning back upon it in acts of interpretation, and by leaping forwards in acts of projection."[6] Jordan's transcendent oratorical moments occur when she balances the idealistic hope of a future unified national community with the pragmatic concerns of everyday life.

At every opportunity, Jordan argues for the reclamation of public values and a revitalized interest in the common good. She encourages "principled pluralism" as a viable alternative to radical individualism and commends values that she believes all citizens hold in common.[7] These values are derived from both public and private domains and are identified as truth, toleration, respect, and community.[8] When Jordan refers to shared values, she has in mind the consistent moral preferences of a diverse populace.

Jordan is not the first to commend shared values. Predecessors and contemporaries such as Lyndon Baines Johnson and Martin Luther King Jr. also offered models of civic mutuality and the enhancement of the common good. In fact, some of their themes resonate in her speeches. However, Jordan's unique contribution to the discussion integrates languages, concepts, and domains that have been perceived as divergent in the public sphere.

In the chapters that follow, key motifs in Jordan's speeches are considered thematically. Each theme is a category that allows Jordan's speeches to be read in a unified way. This unified reading opens the speeches to moral, religious, and evaluative judgments that do not surface when they are critiqued individually.[9] This first chapter offers an introduction to the speeches and their content. Chapter 2 presents her formative years and biographical setting. In Chapter 3, the speeches are situated in the historical context of the Civil Rights movement and the Great Society. Thereafter, I begin an in-depth analysis of the predominant themes in her speeches: ethics, public religion and law.

Chapter 4 examines Jordan's moral categories, the norms and authorities that she deems relevant to her ethics, and her concept of moral fulfillment. In ethics, Jordan identifies the "good" as the collective commitment to social justice and communal well-being. She relates communal flourishing to the revival of public virtue, which is defined as the mutual inclination to moderate self-interest for the good of the community. Finally, Jordan relates this theory of public virtue to public service. She concludes that civic values are not merely abstract ideals, but they are realized in concrete human practices. Jordan considers moral propositions an opportunity for civic discourse that can clarify common goals, for it is through the rhetorical mediations of vested interests that Jordan seeks to disclose emergent shared values. In her view, the growth, development, spirit, and life of her proposed "community of humankind" depend on the identification of those values that can span the ideological chasms of the nation.

Jordan's religious speeches are a surprise to those who remember her as a politician and educator. In Chapter 5, on public religion, she contends that the church and the state are both socially embedded institutions struggling to respond to the needs of humankind. Although Jordan affirms the separation of church and state as a valid constitutional principle, she contends that the metaphors and figures of speech that created the divide have been twisted into a rule of law. As a result, Jordan says an unintended wall has been erected between the "garden of the church" and the "wilderness of the world."[10] She rejects the notion that constitutional protections were meant to be permanent barriers to a dialogue between church and state. In her view, every sector of society including religion must participate in the formation of public policy. In a healthy society, religion can serve as a primary teacher of moral values, a sustainer of local communities, and a catalyst for public accountability.

In Chapter 6, Jordan expresses confidence in the law and in the collective intent of "We the people." Here, the speeches reveal the viability of Jordan's view of justice as fairness, as caring, love, and the foundation for moral fulfillment. For Jordan, law is not relegated exclusively to judicial institutions or restricted to the task of enforcing social and moral propositions. Law remains an integral part of moral discourse. She says, "[T]he rule of law does not ensure justice. Nor does it allow us the easy pastime of avoiding our consciences."[11] Instead, Jordan contends that the law, conjoined with morality and religion, attains heightened relevance in everyday life and thus can contribute to the effectiveness of joint social projects. Moreover, she considers the Constitution to be a dialogical partner in the ongoing public discourse on collective morality and justice.

The discussion of Jordan's interpretation of law as a mediator of cultural discordance leads to the introduction of her model for a national community in Chapter 7. Here, Jordan's ideas about the formation of community are considered and contrasted with

Martin Luther King Jr.'s beloved community and Victor Turner's concept of *communitas*.

It is clear from this brief introduction of themes that Jordan's speeches are a rich repository of her philosophical, political, and religious beliefs and values. Political columnist Molly Ivins captures the clarity of Jordan's speeches when she says: "I think the really stunning thing about [Jordan's] rhetoric was that she used words with the same precision that a master stone mason uses when he makes a wall. She chose words so carefully to build thoughts and never put a word out of place."[12]

Despite Jordan's precision, all speeches are elusive subjects of study because the written artifacts rarely capture nonverbal communication, spontaneous additions to the original text, or the dynamic interaction between listener and speaker that contributes to the meaning. One way to recapture meaning is to view speeches through the lens of rhetorical criticism. Rhetorical critics make use of descriptive, interpretive, and evaluative processes that identify various themes, accents, and emphases that in this instance illuminate Jordan's approach to ethics, public religion, and law.[13] In a more restricted manner, however, I apply Kenneth Burke's dramatistic approach to rhetorical criticism to clarify the motives, substance, and purpose of her speeches. For Burke, an eclectic theorist, the strategic function of rhetoric is "to shape attitudes and induce actions in other human agents."[14]

The use of dramatism as an interpretive tool for Jordan's speeches reveals the world as a space where performance, play, and action define a preexisting and interactive reality. If the world *is* a stage or *is like* a stage — public, participatory, conflictual, and ritualistic — then dramatism lifts the conceptual curtain on the rhetorical motives endemic to that world.[15] The fact that drama and human life experiences share translatable concepts does not diminish either. Nor does the use of a dramatistic methodology to analyze Jordan's speeches imply that the speeches were performed or theatrically contrived. To the contrary, the important categories of ethics, public religion, and law prevalent in Jordan's speeches are particularly amenable to dramatistic analysis. For persons must see their values and faith claims performed ritualistically in order "to induce an emotional belief in them as part of the ultimate meaning of life," says legal theorist Harold Berman.[16] "In the unfolding of life, meaning is not a bequest from culture, socialization or institutional arrangements, nor the realization of either psychological or biological potential. Rather meaning is a continually problematic accomplishment of human interaction."[17]

The language that the speaker selects is the portal through which the rhetorical event connects the public sphere with moral, political, and religious concerns. When I apply these principles to Jordan's speeches, they emerge as a drama of ideas capable of disclosing the motives and social dynamics between persons who share public space and perform socially designated roles. In a manner that Burke commends, I "use all that is there to use," including "planned incongruity," to recapture the elusive motivational processes of Jordan's rhetorical events.[18] Moreover, because this project takes Burke's interdisciplinary approach to rhetorical criticism seriously, I also integrate Victor Turner's theory of liminality and *communitas* into my analysis.[19] Turner's work further delineates Jordan's aesthetic and experiential matrices and contributes to the discussion of her moral formation and public life.

Finally, the speeches offer a glimpse of her elusive and very private life. Recent articles and biographies have claimed a certain "heroism" for Barbara Jordan. She would probably be surprised and a bit perplexed, for she prided herself on her ability to function well in the ordinary context of work, friends, and family, avoiding at all costs the empty symbolism of identity politics.[20] For Jordan, personal achievement is within the reach of every seeker, although the routes to excellence may differ according to differing talents. Because Jordan was ordinary and just like us, we listen to her. Because she was extraordinary when it mattered most, we remember her.

In the chapters that follow, Jordan's speeches tackle the issues that plague and inspire us. I have juxtaposed the voices of Audre Lorde, James Baldwin, Thurgood Marshall, Rabbi Abraham Heschel, bell hooks, and others to create a counterpoint of philosophies and concepts that enrich our understanding of Jordan and her times. Her message to a disillusioned populace is that they need not wait for another political or spiritual exemplar to lead them toward a better life. They can forge that life themselves through an integrative approach to social problem solving and discourse. Jordan practiced what she "preached." Her speeches are a synthesis of ethics, public religion, and law.

Chapter 2

Other Expectations

People always want you to be born where you are. They want
you to have leaped from the womb a public figure. It just
doesn't go that way.   — BARBARA JORDAN[1]

Some public figures internalize the afterglow of fame and national
attention to such an extent that they become one-dimensional
images, reflecting their own hype without substance or spirit.
Jordan escapes that fate by treating fame as just another of
the complexities and contradictions of her personhood. Family,
church, and community influences effectively keep her in touch
with the reality that she is not a self-made woman. In this regard
she says, "I am the composite of my experience and all the people
who had something to do with it."[2] This chapter focuses on the
people and life experiences that influenced Jordan's discourse.

Solid Foundations

Jordan's family enjoyed a stable if not comfortable life in Houston's Fifth Ward despite the economic and racial restrictions imposed by the wider society. Jordan felt nurtured, but admits that
she was a strong-willed child who rebelled against her father's
strict upbringing. She also resisted assumptions about her future
as a wife and mother, for she saw in the lives of female relatives a
confining domesticity that did not appeal to her. Although Jordan
didn't know how to make the transition, she knew that her field of
endeavor would extend beyond the home:

> Now, I thought it unfortunate that the public perceived such
> a neat little box for us, and that in most cases we felt that the

box was right. I thought: The question you have to decide, Barbara Jordan, is whether you're going to fly in the face of what everybody expects out there because you've got your eye someplace else, or whether you can bring the public along to understand that there are some women for whom other expectations are possible.[3]

Those other expectations would be encouraged and nurtured by her maternal grandfather Patten. At an early age, Jordan decides to follow his advice to seek her own levels in the deep and uncharted waters of public life. The two of them were inseparable. Patten encourages her independence and creativity, and teaches her Holy Scripture in a way that relates biblical texts to the ordinary circumstances of life. To be certain, Patten walked to the beat of a different drummer and was given to writing pithy adages and Bible phrases on the tin and cardboard fence that surrounded his junkyard. On the uneven fence rails, he would often sign his name St. John.[4]

Jordan recalls that he taught her to recite the following saying: "Just remember the world is not a playground but a schoolroom. Life is not a holiday but an education. One eternal lesson for us all: to teach us how better we should love."[5] Patten, a man of some entrepreneurial flair, owned several businesses at various times of his life, including a restaurant and a junkyard. Although Jordan prefers working with him, sorting rags and such, to participating in the evening church socials that her sisters enjoyed, she does not miss regular church services or life lessons.

There was more to their relationship than the fun of riding in his wagon and sifting through the junk, the discarded treasures of other people's lives. The junk business provided pocket money, practical business experience, and precious time with her grandfather. She says that Patten communicated in a language that she could understand. His was a narrative way of speaking that she would later claim as her own. Patten taught Jordan to reach beyond attainable objectives toward the limits of her imagination. He accomplished this goal by reinforcing the credo that she had unique qualities and unlimited potential. He would say: "You just trot your own horse and don't get into the same rut as everyone else."[6]

The ruts were all too apparent in the segregated wards of Houston, Texas. When Jordan was growing up, *Plessy v. Ferguson* was the law of the land.[7] From within the nurturing nucleus of the church and family, she learns about the intersecting but mutually exclusive worlds of whites and blacks. However, she does not become philosophically locked into essentialist assumptions about race. In fact, her childhood narrative of segregation provides the basis for a constructive and communal approach to political and moral issues. Jordan also learns that a responsible and ethical existence can be sustained despite racism. This is not to say that either Jordan or her family were unique in their efforts to exemplify human virtue in a problematic and racist social context. To the contrary, their experiences are typical of similarly situated black families of the era.

In her autobiography, Jordan recounts details of a childhood demarcated by unseen color boundaries. Later, in an interview with the *Houston Chronicle* she recalls the following incident: "I recall two water fountains. One marked 'white,' the other marked 'colored.' A friend of my mother's who had very light skin, skin light enough to pass for white, said one day, 'I think I'll drink some white water today.' "[8] In a world where color sometimes mattered more than race, there would be no "passing" for Barbara, no casual sips of "white water." She would have to challenge the status quo on her own terms and in her own dark skin.

It All Matters:
Color, Race, and Body Image

In her autobiography, Jordan recalls one of the sad but important lessons that she learned as a child:

> The world had decided that some of us were more Negro than others.... [T]he whole system ... was saying to us that you achieved more, you went further, you had a better chance ... if you were not black-black with kinky hair. Black was bad, and you didn't want to be black, and so the message was that it was too bad that you were so unfortunate that

your skin was totally black and there was no light there anywhere.[9]

To be born dark and then relegated to a darkness defined as the absence of light would be enough of a burden if it were not for the additional overlay of beauty myths upon the issues of race, gender, and class. A discussion of Jordan's public discourse cannot avoid the historical denigration of black women's voices and bodies. In North America, popular culture and myth have worked together to assign permanent negative values to the color black and specifically to the bodies of black women. bell hooks contributes a poignant example of her own childhood recognition that her color isolated her from the majority culture. hooks says, regarding her sister and herself:

> We talk often about color politics and the ways racism has created an aesthetic that wounds us, a way of thinking about beauty that hurts. In the shadows of late night, we talk about the need to see darkness differently. . . . [W]e long for an aesthetic of blackness — strange and oppositional.[10]

Such an aesthetic as hooks envisions was not available to Jordan. Even as an adult, she was described in denigrating terms by the local media and by some of her colleagues in the Texas legislature. One columnist recalls the obstacles that Jordan encountered:

> She wasn't just black and female, she was homely, she was heavy, and she was dark black. When she first came to the Texas Senate, it was considered a joke to bring racist friends to the gallery. When Barbara Jordan was due to speak, they would no sooner gasp 'Who is that n[—]?' than she would open her mouth and out would roll language Lincoln would have appreciated.[11]

> Aside from the vicarious kick a white lib[eral] can get from watching Jordan speak to a new audience, they tend to snig- ger and assume that anyone who looks that much like a mammy is going to be pretty funny to hear.[12]

Jordan's personal encounters with the rhetoric of oppression are chronicled in the reports of her early years in the Texas legislature:

"One of her colleagues always referred to her as 'the n[—] mammy washer woman."[13] Other reporters proclaimed that she looked like Aunt Jemima but sounded like God. There is an insidious dualism in racist rhetoric. The discourse of racism uses language in a way that splits meaning from motive and relies on the conjunctive nuances of compliment and insult. The quotations that refer to Jordan as a mammy or Aunt Jemima, although putting her on a par with God, are examples of this phenomenon. The social and psychic confusion generated by this discursive incongruity can spawn either inertia or nihilism in the targeted individual or community.[14] Moreover, the energy that it takes to untangle the conjunctives or to expose the malevolence inscribed on the language requires constant and tiring vigilance. Audre Lorde describes the poison that racism emits in the following way:

> Every black woman in America has survived several lifetimes of hatred ... growing up metabolizing hatred like daily bread. Because I am black, because I am a woman, because I am not black enough ... because I am not some particular fantasy of a woman, because I AM. On such a constant diet, one can eventually come to value the hatred of one's enemies more than one values the love of friends. For that hatred becomes the source of anger, and anger is a powerful fuel ... and the catabolic process throws off waste products of fury even when we love.[15]

In this excerpt, Lorde contends that the human soul changes in response to a steady diet of hatred. This statement challenges Jordan's public serenity. One cannot help but wonder, Where is her rage? To some extent, her speeches become an outlet that serves the same purpose as does Lorde's poetry. Some of this catabolic process energizes Jordan's sociopolitical and educational projects, and the remainder is unaccounted for.

Although Jordan is not subsumed with public fury that would hinder her agenda for reconciliation, she struggles to resist racist caricatures. In this respect, bell hooks explains the process of maintaining self and community in the midst of domination. She says, "All colonized people who create an oppositional subculture within the framework of domination recognize that the field of representation (how we see ourselves, how others see us) is a site of ongoing contestation and struggle."[16]

Notwithstanding the struggles, Jordan's healthy self-image acts as a buffer to racial slurs, and she becomes a valued member of the Texas legislature. As for the constant comparisons of Jordan to Aunt Jemima, Jordan herself says, "I would like to refute by my presence...that I look like Aunt Jemima and speak like Ted Kennedy.... [I]t is my contention that I look and speak like Barbara Jordan, a view I might add that is shared by my mother."[17]

It is interesting to note that although the comparison of Jordan to Aunt Jemima was consistent, the standard for comparison changed from God to Ted Kennedy or any other powerful white male. References in these comparisons to God are consistent, for God is seen as a rhetorical surrogate — a divine image of the white male patriarchy. No matter to whom she was compared, when Jordan spoke many people experienced cognitive dissonance. Her image was familiar, but the rhetoric was not. Eventually, the perceived disjuncture between image and voice dissipated, and Jordan was able to unsettle racist assumptions through reasoned and morally inspired rhetoric. Jordan was using the skills and life perspectives taught by her parents and grandparents.

Jordan soon realizes that in some circles, her gender and body image create as many difficulties as does her race. During her years at Phillis Wheatley High School, it becomes apparent that she will not rise above the crowd if that ascent depends on dainty feminine charms. Jordan is a solidly build young woman in a world that values images of female frailty. She wisely chooses to develop her elocution skills and academic prowess and excels as an orator. Later, as a young college coed at Texas Southern University, it became clear that she might be precluded from traveling with the all-male debate team. In response to this threat, biographer Ira Bryant says that she gained weight and cut her hair, "wore flat shoes and sensible clothes." According to Bryant, "Barbara consciously defeminized herself, to create a new no-nonsense image."[18]

Although Jordan does not discuss these decisions in any detail in her autobiography, the positive results are apparent. With weight gain, Jordan escapes from gender boundaries and attains the freedom of movement reserved for men. Recent scholarship identifies the ways in which race, class, and gender intersect to create a multivalent grid of oppression. Upon this grid, Jordan adds the layer of rejection associated with weight gain. Her race afforded her virtual invisibility to the majority culture until she spoke. Her weight affords the same shield even in her own community. Jordan learned her life lessons well. Years in a segregated school system taught her that separate was not equal.[19] Her participation on debate teams taught her that she could level the sociocultural playing field through dialogical engagement. Stories of her grandfather Patten's prison term taught her that the law can be blind to issues of justice.[20] She also learns that her embodiment as a black woman will be a factor in the moral conversation that she has convened. Early on, it becomes apparent that Jordan has taken her grandfather's advice. She is "trotting her own horse" as she journeys toward public life.

A Liminal Journey:
Transcending Essentialisms

Although Jordan is keenly aware of the ways that her experiences as a black woman have affected her life, she responds to issues from any number of combined perspectives in accordance with her own complex self-understandings. In that respect, her oratory differs significantly from the "race conscious" oratory of some of her predecessors. For example, Jordan took every opportunity to remind the nation of the particular plight of African Americans, but she did not claim womanism or feminism or any other gender-specific social location as a vehicle for her discourse. Her speeches evince a belief that there are no special interest virtues. The responsibility to live a principled life accrues to every member of the society, notwithstanding categories of oppression. Jordan insists that excellence is an attainable goal that ameliorates the disadvantages of the oppressed.

One could argue she articulates a moral stance that transcends essentialisms. For example, she speaks to the issues of racial discrimination — taking George Bush to task for his racially

motivated appointment of Clarence Thomas — but she does not
engage with critical race theorists.[21] In addition, she champions
the rights of immigrants, but enigmatically challenges them to
embrace the historically exclusionary common core of American
civic culture.[22] Finally, she attributes her ethics to politically informed interpretations of Christology, but she rejects theological
mysticism.[23]

An initial reaction to Jordan's stance is that she is avoiding her
role as a black spokesperson or is erecting a facade of neutrality and conservatism to shield other agendas.[24] However, Jordan
emerges as a liminal figure "betwixt and between fixed states of
culture."[25] For Victor Turner, a cultural anthropologist, liminality
is described as a fluid state where oppositional concerns are held
in dialectical tension. Life itself becomes such a state, an experiential mix of the secular and sacred, formlessness and structure,
inclusion and exclusion.[26] Jordan's speeches disclose this fluidity.
She draws upon classical theorists such as Aristotle and Alexis
de Tocqueville; however, she also draws from her own personal,
professional, and church experiences. At the hermeneutical level,
Jordan brings new questions and approaches to the task of moral
construction by "occupying new answer positions and questioning
previous suppositions."[27]

Jordan is a black woman on a journey through the uncharted
territories of southern politics. Other crossings follow as Jordan
sojourns in the liminal spaces created by her embodiment. Her
journey is made even more extraordinary by the discourse that she
convenes in public spaces and the conflicted responses that she re-
ceives from a society in transition. Although Jordan's eloquence
affords her a measure of success, she is always in the process of
"becoming." Jordan is not born behind a speaker's platform but
in a segregated section of Houston, Texas. Her transition from
an ordinary "colored girl" in the Fifth Ward to public life as a
spokesperson, politician, and ethicist occurs as a rite of passage.
The transition also requires movement through permeable racial
divisions in the social world. Jordan acknowledges the leap of
consciousness required to move between segregated realms. She remarks that "it seemed an impossibility to make any transition to
the larger world out there."[28]

Turner's theory of liminality helps to contextualize Jordan's emergence as a public speaker. He contends that all rites of passage are marked by the following phases of separation from the familiar, the liminal or threshold experiences, and aggregation or reincorporation into the social whole. The period of separation is marked by a symbolic or physical detachment from a fixed point of familiarity within the social structure. Jordan makes this transition when she goes to Boston University Law School and experiences the temporary loss of her support systems. When she returns to Texas, she is aware of her attenuated or liminal status in society.

Liminality is a state that possesses none of the attributes of the past or the future. Rather, it is an ambiguous and flexible state described in the following passage by Turner:

> Liminal entities are neither here nor there; they are betwixt and between the positions assigned and arrayed by law, custom, convention, and ceremonial. As such, their ambiguous and indeterminate attributes are expressed by a rich variety of symbols in the many societies that ritualize social and cultural transitions. Thus, liminality is frequently likened to death, to being in the womb, to invisibility, to darkness, to bisexuality, to the wilderness, and to an eclipse of the sun or moon.[29]

Turner's description of liminality as a transitional phase is derived from his anthropological work. However, it has applicability beyond that context. First, I suggest that liminality is an apt description of the status of persons who are distanced from society because of immutable traits such as race, ethnicity, or gender. The theory also applies to those who have their social matrix controlled to one extent or another by the dominant social structure. Second, I contend that liminality need not be limited to "darkness" and "eclipse." The invisibility factor that Turner includes in his description of liminality is arguably conducive to an unfettered vantage point. When a person is relatively free of social constraints, life perspectives may be enhanced and movement may be facilitated.

Finally, liminality is seldom a fixed point in the lives of socially or ethnically designated outsiders. Rather, it can be an ebb and flow, a never-ending cycle, and a persistent conceptual overlay upon

other transitions that occur in life. However, I am not assuming that
marginality and liminality are functionally equivalent. Liminality
offers far more positive options, although both evoke images of a
detached state of being apart from the dominant society.

When the society in question is morally diseased (in this instance
by racism, gender bias, and classism), distance is appropriate and
healthy. Such was the case during Jordan's formative years. Primarily, Jordan's "detachment" functions in a positive way, providing
her with the insight necessary to critique the dominant and minority communities.[30] This perspective is evidenced in Jordan's
speeches. More often than not, her rhetoric challenges the status
quo but also seeks the amelioration of differences. However, there
are instances when her detachment creates incongruities in her own
self-perception.

On the one hand, she is aware of her social location and the
impact that the classification poor/black/female has on her life. On
the other hand, she would state after an election defeat that being black and female were neutral characteristics that could not
have affected the outcome. On this particular occasion, Jordan is
told in very specific terms that it will be difficult for her to win
a seat in the Texas legislature: "You have too much going against
you. You're black, you're a woman and you're large. People don't
really like that image."[31] Jordan responds: "I felt that the black
and woman stuff were just side issues, and that people were going
to ignore...those...extraneous issues, that they were neutral."[32]
It is this elusive grasp of self and situation in relation to the world
that evokes the dimmer side of the detachment associated with
liminality.

Poet Audre Lorde writes about the peril of speaking publicly
from liminal spaces. In a brief but poignant excerpt from the
poem "A Litany for Survival," Lorde professes that the rhetoric
of African American women in the public sphere is the affirmation
of self and community despite systematic efforts to render them in-
visible.[33] She says, "When we speak we are afraid our words will
not be heard nor welcomed but when we are silent we are still
afraid. So it is better to speak remembering we were never meant
to survive."[34]

Lorde contends that the act of public proclamation is the only reasonable recourse for those "standing upon the constant edges of decision — crucial and alone."[35] Moreover, she argues that the task of those who are marked for social or physical extinction is to speak the truth as resistance, refutation, and activism. Essentially, Lorde describes the public speech activities of African American foremothers rather than exhorts the use of rhetoric as an unfamiliar practice. Therefore, Jordan can be seen as standing in a long line of women orators from West African griots[36] to Sojourner Truth[37] and Ida B. Wells-Barnett.[38]

Among upwardly mobile blacks, artful enunciation and articulation became the outward symbol of assimilation and acceptability. Having been excluded from mainstream public discourse, African American women of Jordan's era found themselves exercising rhetorical options in the interstices of public life. If you were poor and talented, the way out of poverty was either through the oratory of the church or the courthouse or the statehouse.[39] These seemingly benign efforts toward self-improvement were sustained and encouraged by the black club women.[40] Although recent studies have focused upon the salutary effect that the movement had on race progress, there was another element. The club women modeled some of their values and public rhetoric after the dominant culture. In so doing, they inculcated into the foundational assumptions of their movement a materialism and a bootstrap mentality that would inevitably exacerbate class differences spawned during slavery. Moreover, belonging and acceptability were all too often predicated upon appearance and enunciation. Although these missteps cannot be attributed to Jordan at this juncture, it is clear that a tension exists between her postulation of "excellence" and her recognition of the value of assimilative techniques.

I find that the tension between heartfelt public proclamation and a concern that rhetorical images confirm worthiness evokes Victor Turner's theory of liminality quite appropriately. For Jordan, liminality becomes a positive state that maximizes her individual freedom, for this is a space that is not controlled by the church, the law, ethnic shibboleths, or private interests. It is during her transitory passage to public life that she finds freedom in the spaces that exist in the interstices of the diverging value systems of a pluralistic culture.[41]

Coming to Voice:
A Private Woman in Public Spaces

When Jordan began her public speaking career on the Texas Southern University debate team, she perceived that the private sphere
was the realm of power for white women and the public sphere
was the realm of power for white men. There seemed to be no
niche for her, yet Jordan saw many excluded people struggling to
occupy public spaces. She grew up in a family of accomplished
speakers. Her mother used her oratorical skills in the church, and
both of her grandfathers preached. Jordan acknowledges her own
talent but confesses that she also learned the questionable skill
of "speechifying," defined as oratory with a primary emphasis on
elocution and style rather than content.

While in law school, at Boston University, Jordan realized the
vacuity of this type of discourse and resolved to support her
orality with philosophical and historical information. Evidence of
that effort is seen in her speeches. However, at times her desire
to ground her proclamations with quotations from other sources
almost overwhelms her natural wit and proverbial wisdom.

It is important to note that despite her reputation as an inspiring orator, she is not a part of the informal "talk genre" of the
1990s. Most of her speeches are formal and ceremonial. Most are
delivered during graduation ceremonies and political and religious
gatherings. Although other public speakers routinely blur private
and public boundaries, Jordan engages her audience on a more formal level. She values her own privacy, but recognizes the public
nature of political life. On the issue of privacy, Jordan says, "We
cannot have it both ways. If we choose to be public officials, we
must accept being in the public eye — and we must be willing to
accept public scrutiny."[42]

This statement may seem ironic, given Jordan's penchant for
privacy. Jordan was an intensely private person in an era of media-
driven public curiosity. However, in this quotation, she refers to
the responsibilities that come with the privilege of public service.
It is clear to me after a careful review of her papers that Jordan's
interest in privacy can be attributed, in part, to her choice to be a
facilitator and not the subject of discourse. Although she is willing

to be scrutinized in her public life, she is unwilling to relinquish her privacy. In fact, she would have considered such an intrusion a hindrance to her public goals. For Jordan considers herself a provocateur of the national conscience, a sounding board and proponent of public values. Jordan wants those ideas to be considered on their own merits without reference to personal issues.

As I noted in the Introduction, the power of her rhetoric drew support from all sectors of society. Many groups wanted to claim her as their own. Feminists, black radicals, black conservatives, the religious right, the disabled (after the diagnosis of her neuromuscular disease), gay advocacy groups, and others all wanted her to be a symbol for their causes. They also wanted Jordan to adopt their communities as focal points for her rhetoric. She resists all such claims. "If a mirror is filled with its own reflection, it can reflect nothing else."[43] This metaphor helps to clarify her choice. Jordan refuses to allow the mirror of her personhood to reflect anything other than her public persona.[44]

In the end, we know Jordan through the speeches that serve as a prism of her life and historical context. Her speeches also reflect shifting national concerns, as the values of previous decades are being contested at every level of society. Jordan's speeches chronicle her responses to these transitions and her call for a unity presaged in the founding documents of the nation.

Part Two

The Speeches

Chapter 3

The Speeches
in Historical Context:
The Times They Are "A-Changin' "

The conditions under which we live are rapidly changing, and
the very process of change makes it all the more difficult to
find answers. — BARBARA JORDAN[1]

> Come gather 'round people
> Wherever you roam
> And admit that the waters
> Around you have grown
> And accept it that soon
> You'll be drenched to the bone.
> If your time to you is worth savin'
> Then you better start swimmin'
> Or you'll sink like a stone,
> For the times they are a-changin'
> — BOB DYLAN[2]

Those who consider Bob Dylan the musical guru of an entire generation know that it wasn't because of his melodic voice. It was
because his songs stomped and railed like funky prophets declaring
that the day of revolution had come. Those who consider Barbara
Jordan the ethical guru of this same era must concede that her authority came not from her skill as a trained speaker, but from her
unique ability to engage the hearts and minds of the people. Both
Jordan and Dylan knew that the era of predictability was over. The
times were changing.

Those who came of age during the 1960s and 1970s were accustomed to the rhetoric of grassroots leaders, "social prophets," poets, and liberation theologians. Jordan did not fit into any of these categories; she wasn't even a rank-and-file activist. What could she possibly say to the flower children and their parents now that the visionaries lay dead from assassins' bullets? In the aftermath of assassination, with disillusionment still "blowin' in the wind," Jordan prods the moral imagination of the nation. This is a bold philosophical move. The public square is empty, and debate has dissipated. People are tired of empty political rhetoric, fearful of inspired rhetoric, and unwilling to risk further losses. For despite the years of intense public debate and social action, little has been resolved. Questions as to viable moral ends and the goods that could best serve pluralism are still unanswered. In Burkeian terminology, this was the scene that served as a backdrop for Jordan's speeches. The context is political and moral.

An entire generation seemed to be in shock as it tried to reclaim a culture it had once renounced. In Victor Turner's view, reincorporation of the alienated is the logical conclusion to the journey of an initiate. However, the realities of social stigmatization based on color, class, or gender make the process of aggregation more or less difficult, depending on the circumstances. Turner's discussion emerges from his work with individuals and age-grade societies. However, it is possible that the process of reincorporation is not limited to individuals. Rather, entire generations can find themselves in similar situations. Such was the case in the mid-1970s. When an entire generation attempted to reassume formerly repudiated roles, no one was sure that the feat could be accomplished.

In the midst of this cultural maneuvering, Jordan has the task of articulating a plan that will lead toward moral fulfillment when public expectations of a shared future are at an all-time low. She must also respond to the challenges left by King, Johnson, and Malcolm X as to how a conflicted society can live in peace. In this chapter the speeches are discussed in the context of two major challenges: the Civil Rights movement and Johnson's Great Society.

The Civil Rights Movement

How do you go back to your day job when the strains of "We Shall Overcome" still linger in your ears. The return to business as usual would prove to be as difficult for the nation as it was for the activists. "Everything was changing and nothing was changing."[3] Despite new legislation, the dream of full minority inclusion in North American culture shimmered as a mirage just beyond reach. Jordan comes to national attention after the assassinations of Martin Luther King Jr., Malcolm X, and the deaths and dispersal of the Black Panthers. After King's death, his strategies were being challenged as part of the continuing struggle to determine new directions for the movement.

At its height, the Civil Rights movement and its Christocentric focus assumed that the United States was a "Christian" nation with a spiritual conscience grounded in biblical ethics.[4] In that regard, King's underlying assumption was that a "nation under God" could repent. On the other hand, the Black Nationalist movements assumed that the nation had no conscience where minorities were concerned, but they were unable to push secessionist claims toward completion. Both movements dramatized the national breach between promise and fulfillment.[5]

King, in his Mosaic persona, attempted to wrest the people from racism's pharaonic oppressions through the creative interpretation of biblical and philosophical models of deliverance. His efforts were accompanied by a familiar sermonic cadence, and the songs and spirituals that evolved from slavery accompanied his efforts. King's counterpart, Malcolm X, the quixotic Muslim prophet threatened to purify the social order by refining fire. A stunned nation watched as both moral challenges ended in assassination.

After their deaths, Jordan speaks with a rhetorical cadence of her own and dares the community-at-large to believe earnestly in the rule of law. If it is considered that King and the Black Nationalist movement formed two prongs of the moral trajectory, Jordan's reclamations of constitutional centrism and public virtue formed the third. This is not to say that Jordan's moral interests can be triangulated with Martin's and Malcolm's to form a unified sociopolitical agenda. It is simply to recognize the historical context of her public morality.

Jordan offers an option that does not require moral benevolence or demonizing the majority culture. It requires an examination of constitutional principles, as well as the rhetoric and reality structures of the persons whom the Constitution addresses. Jordan's rhetoric differs from the sermonic discourse and tensive dialogical models of Martin Luther King Jr. and Malcolm X. The leaders of the Civil Rights movement and the insurgent black nationalists focused on the rights of particular segments of society. As a consequence, their rhetoric served as a catalyst to public action and radical social change. In contrast, Jordan's discursive practices emanate from the political supposition that entitlements to a better life are already part of the historical consciousness of the nation and the rule of law. Consequently, her speeches address mutual interests more often than rights. Jordan invites the public to envision a more perfect union; however, she questions whether a union bound by rights rather than shared moral foundations can withstand inevitable cultural shifts.

This is what Jordan says about rights, "I define Rights or a Right as that which is due to anyone by tradition, law, or nature."[6] Jordan admits that this is not a perfect definition because true entitlements emanate from the basic human needs of life, liberty, and the pursuit of happiness. She is aware that despite a bombardment of ideas on the subject, the meaning of public life and public virtue still eludes us. For Jordan, the question is whether the language of rights and duties can dismantle a rampant cultural egocentrism. She says, "The imperative is to do what is right."[7]

The term "right" used in this context is synonymous with responsibility. According to Jordan, the duty of all thinking persons in society is to act in responsible ways. Jordan's rhetoric does not excuse anyone from this duty. To those still dazed by the loss of political idealism that followed the deaths of the Kennedys, she urges a recommitment to civic tasks. To African Americans disillusioned by the deaths of leaders and the quagmire in the courts, she urges a perspectival reflexivity. That is, she encourages the "overcoming" of untenable social circumstances through historical memory, faith in the future, and a realistic sense of self.[8] The task is to conceptualize key moments in the life of the community as part of a historical continuum of understanding, thereby linking present and past. Jordan's speeches suggest that interpretation is something that people undergo and something that each person must do. It is a process of translation whereby the past and present are brought into the same field of understanding. However, many factors such as race and gender and sexuality impact upon interpretive events.

Rhetoric scholar Richard Sennett describes the ways in which interpretive processes are affected by ethnicity and social conditions. He describes the rhetoric of ethnic identity as a human language of displacement, rage, loss, and belonging — highly charged with the pronouns "us" and "them," but infused with a certain optimism.[9] Considering the fact that persons live in a dramatic and socially constructed world, Sennett assumes that ethnicity, rage, and loss have linguistic and textual qualities subject to creative revision.[10]

Jordan also holds out hope for the cultural revisions that will move public discourse from "us and them" to "we." Toward this end she appropriates King's dream language. In fact, Jordan urges her audiences to enter conceptually a realm where they can dream of their own deliverance in terms of individual and communal advancement. Her words are inspiring but infused with reality. This is not the prophetic utterance of King; this is the pragmatic, humanistic vision of Barbara Jordan:

> Dream Big. Dream of skyscrapers and sunken gardens. Dream of unnavigable waters and shallow lakes. Dream of conquest and victory. For if the dream is big enough, chances are that somewhere you will approach what is real for you.[11]

What is real for the reader/listener is the invitation to consider the metaphorical possibilities of a dream that can be reconstructed from the ashes of dissent. It will, of course, be a different dream, one grounded in a shared vision of the world. All of the missing components of mutuality and inclusiveness are reclaimed through the flexible framework of dream language and Jordan's assertion that anyone can accomplish great things if he or she can only imagine small ones.

In later speeches, Jordan reprises the dream theme. In an address entitled "A Wake-up Call for the American Dream" Jordan begins with the welcoming pronoun "us." She says, "No one can match *us* in extolling, celebrating, and lauding over others

this thing...we call the American Dream."[12] The speech to a
high school group in Memphis, Tennessee, assumes that a dream
pronounced dead when King was killed in Memphis, lives.

Notwithstanding this dream language, Jordan is a realist. She
quotes statistics, makes historical references, and connects symbolic concepts to factually expository language. In 1990, the
dreams of which she speaks are not yet a reality. Who then is
the *us* to whom she refers in the Memphis speech? It seems that
Jordan performs an act that she urges her audience to perform.
Using symbolism, moral imperatives, and historical imagination as
complementary rhetorical devices, she creatively imagines a state
of national harmony that is yet to occur.

Repeating a phrase from her famous Watergate speech, Jordan reminds the high school students that they were not included
in the founding documents of the country. She moves from the
imaginative "us" to the historical "we" as she documents the
legislative and judicial path to inclusion. She acknowledges the special difficulties that ensue from racism, such as inadequate health
care and poverty. However, she urges unrelenting efforts toward
ameliorating the problems. This is the challenge that she issues:

> The American Dream is not dead. It is at rest for many of
> you. Your challenge and your opportunity is to issue a very
> loud wake-up call. You must challenge all prophets of doom
> and defeat. With unrelenting determination you must make
> the American Dream live for you. But how, you may say?
> I suggest that you start by refusing to accept your present
> conditions as a permanent condition....Believe that change
> is possible....Believe in yourself first....Recast the Ameri-
> can Dream and make it yours. African/Black Americans are
> neither strangers nor guests here. This is our country, and we
> fully intend to make it work for us.[13]

Jordan ends with the provocative "us." It is clear that she is
provoking the audience to consider their status and define their
expectations. The prevailing theme emphasizes the agent-act relationship. Her call to defeat the "prophets of doom" has a
fascinating double meaning. Here, she refers metaphorically to the
media pundits and political commentators, but prophets are also

representatives of divine will. Essentially, she argues that the plight of the excluded, whether of divine or secular origins, can be reversed. She begins the language of reversal with words associated with faith. Several times she repeats the word "believe," but she does not stop there. For Jordan, belief and action are the means toward an end. She identifies that end as full inclusion in the national "us" or "We the people."

In her "Who Speaks for the Negro?" speech (written soon after King's death) Jordan's comments are couched in the language of promise and fulfillment. She says: "We are trying to define America, to affirm and actualize its promise .... [A] promise is not made in a vacuum in air or to land and water. A promise is made to a person, a responding, expecting person. This country made an historical promise to a people, a responding, expecting people.[14]

The argument is clear and incisive. The nation contends that African Americans are not entitled to participate fully in public life, yet through laws and historical documents a promise of freedom and equality is made. Jordan implies that the promise is prima facie recognition of black personhood. She also looks to public theologian Reinhold Niebuhr to support her theory that racism is an aberration that obstructs efforts to achieve consensus about the common good. According to Niebuhr:

> The sense of racial superiority means that a particular kind of man, white or black, Jew or Gentile, Occidental or Oriental, forgets the conditioned character of his life and culture and pretends that his color, creed or culture represents some kind of final and absolute criterion of the good. This is a pathetic and dangerous fallacy.... [I]t cannot be cured merely by a shift in a given social equilibrium. It can be mitigated by education programs designed to reveal the relative character of all human cultures and the excellencies in forms of life other than our own.[15]

Jordan shares Niebuhr's concerns and his pessimism about the current state of American culture. This is her rather surprising language: "No nation can, overnight, shed a prejudice ingrained for three hundred years — years in which the Negro always has been an alien creature, with an alien skin, in an alien world."[16] This language is not the conservative, flag-waving rhetoric of the Barbara Jordan who has become a cultural icon. In this speech, Jordan calls for radical surgery, a cutting away of the social disorder that threatens to destroy the body politic.

Jordan's concerns are not limited to the status of minorities.[17] She believes that a successful society depends on the contributions of all of its constituents. Moreover, she knows that the protests of minorities only hint at the deeper discontent and seeds of public conflict sedimented deep within the nation's historical consciousness. For this reason, well-meaning attempts to transform the social order have unraveled. The remaining options are untenable: violence, a retreat from the dialogue of pluralism into nihilism, and the politics of greed and self-interest. Jordan must encourage her listeners to salvage the disintegrating reality that they have inherited. To more clearly discern the effectiveness of Jordan's proposals, it is helpful to juxtapose a contemporary who experiences the same issues of race and gender yet approaches cultural criticism in a completely different fashion. That person is James Baldwin, playwright, child preacher, novelist, and cultural critic. Baldwin offers poignant assessments of the social system that Jordan tries to salvage. As such, he provides an interesting counterpart to Jordan's position.[18] Baldwin challenges the liberal belief that blacks will become "just another ethnic group" in America after the ideals of the Civil Rights movement become practical realities.[19]

Unlike Jordan, who ascribes to the prevailing liberal mantra of integration as an expression of civic humanism, Baldwin asserts the moral disgust of the African American community with the majority culture.[20] His exposition of the love/hate dichotomy and subliminal rage of an entire race was unsettling and prophetic. Jordan says this about Baldwin's work:

> James Baldwin, a Negro author has written of the Negro: "You were born where you were born and faced the future you faced because you were black and for no other reason. You were born into a society which spelled out with brutal clarity and in as many ways as possible that you were a worthless human being."[21]

Jordan continues in her own words:

> The struggle of the Negro could be described as a valiant effort to overcome the last vestiges of invisibility and an accompanying effort to secure his [her] individuality, his [her] wholeness, and relevance as a human being.[22]

Baldwin's rhetoric is tinged with rage and despair. Jordan considers rage counterproductive and urges estranged Americans to engage in meaningful and moral participation in politics and public life. Her emphasis is upon humanity as an aggregate rather than an essentialist category. In this passage, it is important to note that her references to invisibility should not be considered synonymous with liminality. Although it is true that liminality presumes fluidity and personal or metaphorical distance from society, some level of self-awareness grounds the concept. The invisibility to which she refers hints at a cognitive distortion, an absence of self-awareness and connection to others.

When James Baldwin speaks about the moral context of the African American community, his tone is prophetic. However, he has lost faith in the ability of the general populace to act on behalf of the common good, without limiting that good to the privileged majority. Jordan believes that moral flourishing is possible if persons develop an internal moral sensibility to order external choices. Although they take different approaches, both Jordan and Baldwin creatively challenge the existing social order from a liminal context, moving in and out of rhetorically dynamic zones.

Accordingly, Jordan's response to the end of the Civil Rights movement is to urge ethnic minorities to resist rebellion's intoxicating lure in favor of moral agency. Jordan urges minorities to eschew empty rhetoric about dignity and to be men and women of dignity. She urges them to look deeply into their inner being to determine who they are and what they want out of life: "Your society has given you a setting in which to develop! It may not be of your making, or to your liking, but you're stuck with it."[23]

Jordan uses this speech to describe a few minority options. Malcolm X and Martin Luther King Jr. have emphasized the oppressive nature of segregation and the plight of African Americans as victims of discrimination. Jordan acknowledges discrimination as one aspect of the social scene. However, she broadens its effects to include a "new discrimination," not based on race or ethnicity, but against those who lack the skills, education, or will to claim their own well-being. She asks this salient question, "Will you become a victim of the New Discrimination?"[24]

Jordan challenges African Americans on two fronts: (1) to acquire an education that will allow them to function in an age of science and technology; (2) to develop a middle class that is historically relevant, culturally grounded, and not a carbon copy of Anglicized class structures. Jordan believes that responsible educated citizens are indispensable to a democracy.[25] In fact, Jordan connects responsibility and rights to education. The problem is that she cannot have it both ways. Like John Stuart Mill and Aristotle, she seems to propose a formula that requires virtue plus education to reach the goal of moral fulfillment. In earlier speeches, she uses language that could lead one to conclude that success and economic empowerment supercede virtue in the equation. At the Black Expo in Indiana, she clarifies her views on education for the African American community:

> Education remains the ticket to success in the majority community. Education is the ticket out — the ticket out of lives that have no hope of fulfilling their potential. Education is the ticket that will provide a black student with the sense that he or she can make it in the world.[26]

Compare Jordan's and James Baldwin's commentary on the role that education should play in the African American community. For Baldwin:

> The purpose of education finally is to create in a person the ability to look at the world...to make [her] his own decisions, to say...this is black or this is white, to decide... whether there is a God in heaven or not. To ask questions of the universe and then to learn to live with those questions is the way [s]he achieves [her] his own identity.[27]

Baldwin emphasizes education as an enhancement to social and personal perspectives, whereas Jordan focuses on education as the vehicle that will transport people out of the house of bondage to a realm of freedom and opportunity. Taken in the context of her other speeches, it is likely that Jordan seeks a balance between moral ideals and practical applications of moral theory to an issue such as education.

Jordan believes that the Civil Rights movement can be fulfilled through a multiethnic commitment to excellence and a shared destiny. She has witnessed the successes and failures of both the Civil Rights movement and Johnson's Great Society and is not deterred from her goals. Jordan is rhetorically constructing the foundations for this future community because she believes that a truly great society is just within reach.

The Great Society

As the Civil Rights movement wound down, some hoped that Lyndon Johnson's initiatives would stabilize the social order. Jordan watched her fellow Texan, Lyndon Johnson, attempt to redirect legislative history toward that end. Bills that had been mired in red tape on President Kennedy's watch suddenly surfaced and became the law of the land. It was assumed that the "Great Society" would eradicate decades of racism and economic marginalization. Johnson was funding programs to reverse objective manifestations of inequality. However, as history would record, assassinations and social unrest provide poor soil for the sustenance of nascent social projects. Moreover, there was a war going on in a country that was relatively unknown to most Americans. When Vietnam simmered to a boil, Johnson's Great Society would be no match for the body count reported each night on the evening news.

Johnson is a friend and political mentor to Jordan. However, as her political fortunes rise, his decline. As a consequence, twenty years after his administration ends, little serious thought has been given to the impact of his social policies on the nation.[28] Jordan's speeches on Johnson and the Great Society depict the man and his mission as purveyors of hope. In a speech given at the University of Michigan, Johnson asks for the imagination, initiative, and indignation of the public to move the country toward moral flourishing.[29] Jordan argues that Johnson's call for public morality is indicative of his internal moral compass and keen political instincts.

In a keynote address given at Hofstra University on April 10, 1986, Jordan offers an insightful retrospective of Johnson, presenting him as a man of moral depth.[30] In Jordan's speeches, Johnson is depicted as a patriot (using the language of law, constitutionalism, and liberty); a servant of the public and "quintessential" Texan (using the language of moral conscience); and a man who integrated his religious sensibilities with his politics (using the language of public religion). However, a politician who suffers a loss of public image and public confidence, as Johnson did during the Vietnam war, cannot be described using the usual political rhetoric. Consequently, Jordan astutely conjoins her references to Johnson's patriotism with specificity about his moral acts.[31] In Jordan's discourse, Johnson becomes a participant in the ordinary substance of life who does not retreat from difficult choices.

To create the identification with her audience, she begins by acknowledging Johnson's Texas-sized foibles and "larger than life" image that her audience knows too well. She describes him as a "servant of the public," but admits that "his actions were not always applauded by his fellow Texans or non-Texans. Notwithstanding that fact of political life, he acted. A Texan? Yes. An uncommon Texan? Sometimes, sometimes."[32]

Jordan adopts "truth" as a site of mutual understanding. Although identifying Johnson's exemplary traits, she hints at his missteps and failures. In so doing, she establishes her own credibility and then exposes her own limitations within the discourse. Jordan realizes that her audience will assume certain political allegiances that might compromise an honest opinion. However, when Jordan is acting politically, she gives clear signals to that effect. Her speeches about Johnson and his legacy do not emphasize his political acumen; rather, it is his commitment to achievable societal goals that intrigues her.

Of Johnson she says: "His voice many times blended harmoniously with the voice of the people. But when the voices of those who were out of sync with liberty became loud, one could hear Lyndon Johnson's invocation of Isaiah's invocation, 'come now, let us reason together.'"[33] Here, Jordan compares Johnson's human endeavor with the discourse of faith. To reason as Isaiah reasons is to speak the language of covenantal memory, vision, and purpose to those who suffer.[34] Jordan also presents Johnson not only as a powerful former president, but also as the paradigm of the common citizen with traits that she can commend: patriotism, morality, and faith.

Finally, she lifts up Johnson's presidency as visionary. Actually, it is not unusual in Jordan's speeches to find an eclectic mix of the ordinary and the ideal:

> Vision is a requirement of leadership. Without it one becomes mired in the present with no clue about goals, ends, or future. A lack of vision gives support to whatever negatives this present moment embraces. If the society allows existing wrongs to go unchallenged, the impression is created that such wrongs have the support of the majority, and, as a consequence, they sail unchallenged into the future.[35]

In this speech, Jordan juxtaposes Johnson, George Bush, and King Solomon as three models of leadership. Johnson assumes the role of the visionary, Bush the buffoon, and Solomon a source of sagacious counsel. According to Jordan, Bush fares so poorly in this comparison because of his lack of vision. She says, "The current President has reduced — demoted — vision to prime time material for comics and Saturday Night Live productions." She continues, "In an offhanded and inappropriate manner, he speaks of that 'vision thing. . . .' We pay a price for treating vision as a joke. It is a serious matter."[36]

In retrospect, one could conclude that the lampooning of Bush in late-night satiric skits had more to do with national discontent with his administration than with any one failure on his part. However, in this speech, Jordan depicts Bush as fodder for comedians. He is also a dramatic foil who helps Jordan reinterpret Johnson's initiatives. What Jordan leaves unsaid is that Johnson was also lampooned by the rapier wit of television satirists.

Jordan concludes that a great effort toward social equality ended with the demise of the Great Society. However, the ideal of a unified and responsible social project continues to undergird her own moral agenda. This is not to imply that her ethical mandates

were derived from the Johnson initiatives. Jordan's moral philosophy is uniquely her own. It is to recount the anomalies of history
that juxtapose two people from the same locale, with the same de-
termination to challenge the status quo and affect the future of a
nation.

On the twentieth anniversary of the Great Society, Jordan admits that the project had been excessive in scope. However, she
continues to believe in the moral objectives that framed the ideals.
Johnson would have agreed with her. On one occasion he said:
"The Great Society is not a safe harbor, a resting place, a final
objective, a finished work. It is a challenge constantly renewed,
beckoning us toward a destiny where the meaning of our lives
matches the marvelous products of our labor."[37] What wonderful
images this language evokes! It is now Jordan's turn to respond to
the call of destiny.

Part Three

The Themes

Chapter 4

Ethics: Here Be Dragons

The world looks to us as the leader of the free world to restore sanity to the conduct of the people of the world. The
house of America must be put in order.... The earth is too
small, in too much turmoil for us to do otherwise.

— Barbara Jordan[1]

Ancient maps of the world — when the world was flat — inform us concerning that void where America was waiting to
be discovered, HERE BE DRAGONS. Dragons may not have
been here then, but they are certainly here now, breathing
fire, belching smoke; or, to be less literary and biblical about
it, attempting to intimidate the mores, morals, and morality
of this particular and peculiar time and place.

— James Baldwin[2]

Washington, D.C., is hardly a haven of prehistoric monsters. Yet,
in retrospect, Baldwin's warning to his generation seems timely
and loving. For when Jordan arrived in the nation's capital as
the first black woman to be elected to Congress from the South
since Reconstruction, the mythic beasts lurked. No longer breathing fire, they engaged political visionaries in exhausting skirmishes
undaunted by their credentials or bravado. Jordan soon staked a
claim to high moral ground, a site she would not soon relinquish.

Chapters 2 and 3 introduced Barbara Jordan and her speeches
in their cultural and historical context. In this chapter, I explore
Jordan's ethics as an important theme in her speeches. The discussion focuses on her particular moral context, the values that
function as norms and authorities within that context, and her vision of moral fulfillment. Because Jordan considers ethics to be an
integral part of everyday life, her speeches raise basic questions

about morality. Why be moral? Why show tolerance, respect, or love for other human beings? Are there particular social circumstances that trigger moral accountability? Jordan is not the first to grapple with these questions.[3] However, her speeches offer a pragmatic response. For Jordan, the failure to agree upon foundational moral principles dooms any social project to inevitable failure. Moreover, moral agency constitutes more than connective tissue for cooperative projects; it defines human experience.

Jordan says: "How do you judge if an action might be unethical? ... Your entire life experience informs, nurtures, and tutors your ethical instincts."[4] She also says: "Our lives are the aggregate of all we have experienced. These experiences have caused us to form judgments, ideas, tilts, and taints."[5] Amid the tilts and taints, Jordan derives resolute moral sensibilities from rich and complex life experiences. She also incorporates basic tenets from the study of moral philosophy into her theoretical framework. Although Jordan succeeds in politics, teaching, and law, she grounds her practices in ethics. Jordan contends that an ethical person can be described as one who discerns right from wrong and is an integral part of a community that mutually resolves disputes that arise from conflicting values.[6]

Jordan's speeches disclose her own moral inclinations. Over time, the public learns that she is a person who surveys the moral landscape, assessing the "ought," the "is," and the potential for transcendence. Then she embarks upon a consistent moral approach to recurring social problems. Like scenes in a play, her speeches depict civic life as an ongoing moral project linked to historical, religious, and political processes.[7]

The following activities are identified by Jordan as crucial contributors to public life: public discourse as an integral part of the sociopolitical process; individual responsibility and community service; the development of public virtue; and finally a concern for the common good. These activities require some level of consensus. They also require a guiding ethics to facilitate moral judgments and to govern social conduct by providing consistent references to objective moral standards. Whether or not Jordan's moral standards meet the test of objectivity and consistence will be considered for years to come. Certainly, she proposes a viable concept of moral flourishing as a desirable end. However, the means to that end must still be debated.

At this point, a working definition of ethics facilitates the discussion. Because ethics belongs to all realms and none, it is sometimes difficult to determine the distinguishing characteristics of the moral domain. Philosopher and ethicist Victor Anderson's definition of ethics is precise and applicable:

> Ethics is the study of morally relevant human actions, the conditions under which we can pass judgments on such actions, and our ability to make judgments whether our actions can be commended to others for public acceptance. Ethics studies the processes of moral discernment and action.[8]

Anderson's approach to ethics does not burden moral science with the language of prohibition — what ought or ought not be done. Instead, he emphasizes the spark of intuitiveness that he refers to as moral discernment. I interpret Anderson's references to moral discernment as an alertness of spirit and mind such that all of the human capacities of moral imagination, reasoning, spirituality, and experience are brought to bear upon the task of prioritizing values. The word *discernment* also sends a message that allows an "ethics of the everyday" to share space with abstract theorizing.[9]

Jordan's approach to ethics comports with this definition. Her moral instincts function as moral discernments that initiate informed and morally relevant choices. She possesses certain competencies that enhance her moral discernment. First, she is familiar with the rules that govern the social order. Second, she is able to identify the values that will enhance community life. Finally, she chooses means that are congruent with the ends sought.[10] The fact that Jordan acquires these competencies, despite the influences of inconsistent and often conflicting "goods" identified by segregated social realms, speaks to the effectiveness of her moral judgments. Ultimately, moral discernment is nurtured internally and tested in public forums.

It is one thing to determine that moral discernment and action are the essential elements of ethics. It is quite another to assess contextually those tasks. Moral discernment takes on an entirely different nuance when all of the values that have governed society are called into question. Watergate became the first public test of Jordan's ethics.

Watergate — In the Absence of Virtue

Today the events surrounding Watergate seem quaint and distant. However, when the scandal broke, it was a watershed event, a national loss of innocence. In comparison, the laissez faire responses of the nation to the impeachment hearings of William Jefferson Clinton bear little resemblance to the events that catapulted Jordan into national focus. Watergate was a morality play of epic proportions, a conspiracy drama with all of the legendary elements of intrigue, public outrage, and revelation. What began as a botched burglary ended up as a cover-up that unraveled Nixon's presidency and exposed a barrenness at the core of political ethics. A national moral crisis ensued.[11]

America was experiencing a shift in its collective consciousness and the distortion of an important national myth. This myth assumed that success and progress would be accompanied by virtue. Watergate supplanted this assumption and substituted a mantra of greed and inverted priorities. As the scandal ran its course, citizens who had carefully maintained a naiveté about the workings of government were bombarded by news of political manipulations that began at the White House.

But the most unsettling occurrence was an act of omission rather than commission. A basic tenet of political survival was forgotten — that representative democracies must model the values held dear by the people if they are to maintain legitimate authority. Quoting Thomas Jefferson, Jordan says: "It may have been forgotten by the Nixon administration. It is logical, simple, and true. The public official who is a moral [person] knows [that]...the whole art of government consists in the art of being honest."[12]

Jordan was often asked to reprise her analysis of the scandal, for it was the event that defined her career and introduced the nation to her ethics. Before she delivered her televised speech before the House Judiciary Committee, few people outside of Texas knew her name. When the speech was over, Jordan's name was a household word. In her Watergate speech, Jordan situates herself as a protagonist who symbolically stands for national ideals in opposition to rampant abuses of political power. The speech positions her as an emblematic figure, the outsider heroine who speaks the unspeakable and acts as a focal point for public opinion and moral discourse.

Cultural theorist Michel Maffesoli explains the difference between political types who rhetorically delineate the path to follow and symbolic or mythic types who act as "pure containers" for collective sensibilities. The sole purpose for the latter type is to capture and restate the collective spirit at a precise moment in time.[13] Jordan falls into the latter category. In Burkeian terms, she is the moral agent in the Watergate speech who represents the public interest and symbolically upholds democratic ideals.

Jordan assumes this role in her most famous speech, "Opening Statement to the House Judiciary Committee Proceedings on [the] Impeachment of Richard Nixon."[14] Here she addresses the lack of individual and collective virtue in Nixon's administration and compares the vacuous rhetoric of renegade, political power brokers with the values of the people. Her remarks on the impending impeachment of Nixon were acclaimed for their effectiveness and power as she delineated the boundaries of public virtue.

As she mobilizes public opinion, defining and eliciting the shared moral outrage of the nation, she solidifies the responses of an unseen national audience. Elements of Burke's pentad can be identified in this speech.[15] By including an analysis of the act — impeachment — and the interaction of two agents — the House Judiciary Committee and Richard Nixon — she diminishes the sense that impeachment is being used as a political vendetta. It is crucial that this speech establish a sense of neutrality and distance from party partisanship. After all, it is the overzealousness of misanthrope politicians who have caused the Watergate fiasco. Jordan achieves this sense of neutrality and rhetorical distance by emphasizing her outsider status as an African American female junior member of the committee.[16]

Because Jordan is fully aware of the impact that her race will have on her remarks, she addresses this issue first. She begins by noting that amendments to the Constitution and court decisions have afforded minorities full status as citizens. However, the very fact that she is the first black female representative from Texas since Reconstruction is proof of the tenuousness of that status. Despite advancements, Jordan remains a novelty in American government. She says:

> Earlier today we heard the beginning of the preamble to the Constitution of the United States, "We the people." It is a very eloquent beginning. But when that document was completed, on the seventeenth of September in 1787, I was not included in "We the people." I felt somehow for many years that George Washington and Alexander Hamilton just left me out by mistake. But through the process of amendment, interpretation, and court decision, I have finally been included in "We the people.[17]

With regard to the similar exclusion of women, she says in a later speech: "One may ask whether the founders were mean-spirited and just didn't like women? The answer is no. They loved women but had a very limited 18th-century notion about their role in the world."[18] Few would disagree that the Constitution, though visionary in some respects, reflects the ethos of its era. Justice Roger B. Taney affirms the exclusionary intent of the framers in the following passage taken from the *Dred Scott* case. With reference to African Americans, Justice Taney said:

> We think they are not included and were never intended to be included. . . . They had for more than a century before been regarded as being of an inferior order, and altogether unfit to associate with the white race . . . and so far inferior that they had no rights which the white man was bound to respect. . . . Accordingly, a Negro of the African race was regarded . . . as an article of property, and held and bought and sold as such. . . . No one seems to have doubted the correctness of the prevailing opinion of the time.[19]

The fact that African Americans and women were excluded from the Constitutional Preamble "We the people" stands in stark contrast to the authority that Jordan exercises. However, before she challenges the highest governmental powers, she creates an identification with the listener by claiming her own cultural identity. This is necessary, lest anyone think that her competence distances her from her ethnicity. She is aware that her speaking style and knowledge of constitutional issues have always been considered by the majority culture to be incongruous with its conflicted image of the African American female. Now, Jordan, once ridiculed, becomes the focal point for national agreement.

When she says "I was not included," she is the voice of the African American community to the nation. Then, acting in a representative capacity, she symbolically dons the mantle of constitutional protections. Once this identification is made, she can represent the interests of the entire body politic with full authority. The rhetorical evidence of her wider representative capacity occurs when she substitutes the collective "we" for her prefatory use of the inquisitors pronoun "I."[20] She is now spokesperson for the nation's citizenry.

As the speech continues, Jordan teaches constitutional lessons and puts Nixon's deeds on the rhetorical witness stand; she allows the criteria for impeachment to cross examine, as if a case against him is being tried. Jordan builds her case with specificity and a formal neutrality until she reaches a shocking conclusion. After explicating allegations that Nixon has abused his power by obtaining information about political enemies through the CIA, FBI, and IRS, Jordan sheds her neutral stance to become a moral advocate. In this role, she expresses her willingness to relinquish the Constitution to a paper shredder if the impeachment provision cannot reach the offenses of the president.

Her indignation is fueled by her belief that the Constitution is a "sacred" text worthy of her faith and partisan advocacy. Despite her reverence for the document, she sanctions its metaphorical destruction during her speech before the Judiciary Committee, but only for limited reasons. The shredding of the Constitution is not warranted because of its racially exclusionary origins or because it has been used on occasion to justify political ends. Such a fate is only justified if the document fails to protect the moral foundations of the nation. Jordan wants protection for the specified and unspecified moral tenets incorporated into the clauses and penumbras of the Constitution.[21] The willful violation of cultural norms makes

Jordan angry. In contrast to Nixon's characterization of Watergate as the "thinnest scandal," Jordan considers it a precursor to moral decline.

Jordan asks citizens to garner their moral sensibilities and determine the tenor of public life. Although it seems that the legislators and professionals are controlling outcomes, she insists that moral power remains in the hands of the people. She continues by making the connection between accountability and the spiritual recovery of the nation. She says, "Only when men and women in government are accountable to the citizenry, accountable morally, accountable to the Constitution, will inflation, disruption, and discontent be solved and the spirit restored."[22] Accountability becomes an important, covenantal, and formal measure of Jordan's public morality. Once this standard has been established, Jordan allows listeners to reach their own conclusions as to whether the standards for impeachment have been met. She is certain that the American people can and will draw reasonable conclusions as to Nixon's culpability.

It is important to note that when Jordan speaks to and for the people of the nation, she is speaking on more than one level. Jordan has taken no opinion polls and consequently has no way of knowing whether she speaks for the majority of Americans. Nevertheless she can rhetorically construct an assenting moral community to act as a proxy for the citizenry.[23] By the end of her Watergate speech, impeachment is probable. Nixon's subsequent resignation is prompted as much by a firestorm of negative public opinion as it is by his own missteps.

Jordan's moral indignation about Watergate is expressed in several speeches. In each, she declares that government must be a primary moral exemplar, for when government fails, civil liberties are at risk. However, she also wants the nation to know that not all of the problems of Watergate can be attributed to Nixon. She argues that nothing can protect the nation from "moral ineptitude." She continues:

> Decency, integrity, honor, honesty, these cannot be legislated. The Congress is ill-equipped to amend the Ten Commandments, and should it try, it would probably create some loopholes which are not there now. . . . And yet the torment

of Watergate is a sign to us all. We have both the capacity and the will to act within our democratic institutions to right our wrongs.[24]

Jordan believes that the people still have the capability of determining the parameters of public virtue. In her "Moving on from Watergate" speech, Jordan models a prospective optimism. She suggests that the scandals of Watergate may have spawned unlikely results: an attention to issues of accountability in government, and the launching of investigations that will ultimately reduce the opportunities for abuses of power. Unfortunately, Jordan's hunch is incorrect. History inevitably repeats itself. In a speech entitled "Watergate and Irangate, or Arrogance and Ignorance," Jordan compares the activities of Nixon and Ronald Reagan.[25] Although she concludes that the Iran Contra and Watergate situations differ significantly, there is a connection, a lack of trust between the people and the presidents who represent their interests. A stable democracy is built on the fair implementation of law and a moral as well as social covenant between the people and their representatives. She says: "We began our nation as a reaction to an abusive parent. We wrote safeguards into our system of government to protect [it] from the concentration of power into tyrannical hands."[26] For Jordan, the most important safeguard is the right of the people to challenge moral aberrance and to declare their values.

Intergenerational Values

Jordan contends that virtue is not only a moral trait; it is also a normative standard capable of benefiting both the individual and the community. She defines norms as shared understandings, rules, expectations or values, and concerns that under optimal circumstances can stabilize social interactions and create governing standards.[27] Theologian Hans Küng highlights the importance of agreement upon normative standards when he says, "Without a minimal basic consensus on certain values, norms, and attitudes, no human society worth living in is possible. Even a modern democracy cannot function without such a basic consensus, which constantly has to be rediscovered in dialogue."[28]

In an era when moral language is primarily the language of dissension and paradox, Jordan's speeches propose resolute values. She considers common values to be generative, a legacy of one generation to another and a microcosm of the moral benchmarks of the era. Accordingly, she says, each generation leaves as a legacy to the future, "its best institutions, its highest ideals, the most enduring of values. This expectation exists because there is a continuum of reciprocal rights, duties, and obligations. Those reciprocal duties . . . continue without ceasing."[29]

Once again, Jordan uses the language of rights; however, this time she argues that successor generations can expect a legacy of moral languages and norms from predecessors who have actively sought the common good. Jordan suggests that these norms are derived from moral sensibilities inculcated into personal relationships and reflected in codified moral prescriptions.[30] Rights and duties, virtues and values offer a relatively complete picture of our moral choices. Of course, there are differences between external controls and internal guidelines, and on occasion, one or the other may predominate. However, Jordan believes these spheres of moral endeavor should enhance rather than displace one another.

In a commencement speech to law students graduating from the University of Louisville, Jordan delineates the characteristics of the moral agent. Using Reinhold Niebuhr's *Moral Man and Immoral Society* as a narrative foil, she concludes that public service is the quintessential proof that shared values and individual responsibility rather than greed, avarice, and selfishness epitomize human nature.[31] She is convinced that even if Niebuhr's assessment of human nature is correct, transcendence is always possible.

In her "Universalization" speech, Jordan fleshes out her concept of morality by creating a linkage with basic kindergarten rules. Quoting Robert Fulghum's popular book of life rules gleaned from kindergarten, Jordan reduces ethics to the following precepts: don't hit, but share, hold hands in public, and live a balanced life.[32] She addresses graduating law students who are accustomed to complexity. Therefore, she oversimplifies. However, her point is clear: Moral sentiments are not complicated or abstract. They are personal principles that guide and constrain our public and private lives, and they are the same principles that undergird our democratic institutions. Thus there is a moral nexus between institutions with the delegated authority to act as proxies for the public will and private individuals. She characterizes morality as a distinctly personal code of conduct expressed in public ways.

Jordan is unwilling to relegate ethics to statutory prescriptions, "liability insurance" for professionals, or an amorphous configuration of public expectations. She is aware of the dilemma of the moral sciences, fueled by the increasing lack of agreement on objective moral standards. Her response to rampant relativism is a return to virtue ethics and the claim that agreement can be reached as to basic goods if commonly held values become foundational in public and private life.

The moral inheritance that Jordan speaks of can accrue only in a society that values intentional moral activities. Such activities assume the exercise of free will in concert with other equally free beings. Toward that end, liberty and justice are crucial. In a Western context, the terms "liberty" and "justice" have richly layered meanings. Jordan does not depict these principles as abstract theoretical concepts. Rather, she identifies them as prerequisite values necessary for the development of mutuality. In turn, mutuality engenders common values.

Jordan believes that commendable moral behavior is associated with the consistent and voluntary exemplification of such virtues as truthfulness, respect, courage, toleration, and responsibility. These virtues are more than commendable moral traits. They are the norms that should guide the moral life. In essence, she argues that the rights and duties of a free populace ensure the freedoms necessary to nurture these norms.

Jordan's ideal moral constructs embody the goals and ends of past and future generations. She values continuity in the public domain and struggles with the concept of immutable moral standards. She is clearly conflicted as to whether society would be better served by dynamic norms that reflect differences in social, religious, and legal perspectives, or by those that remain the same.[33]

Her pursuit of reliable, intergenerational norms leads to the

development of her theory of "conviction values." In a commencement speech before the University of Texas, she defines conviction
values as "firmly fixed, unwavering and immutable; that there are
some traits of character which are or should be non-negotiable;
that we should have a set of beliefs which is endemic to our concept of self." Jordan continues: "The values, which I have in mind,
are those which should be universally agreed upon because they
foster a sense of community: they are healing and civilizing. They
promote the general welfare and the common good. Those values
include education, kindness, justice, and responsibility."[34]

Jordan entices the listener into the safe milieu of moral constancy that conviction values would provide and then challenges
the connotation that constancy is synonymous with good. In fact,
she draws clear distinctions between values that are reliable and
values that are inflexible. She says, "If convictions cause one to
be rigid, inflexible, and unwilling to compromise when compromise is necessary, such convictions do not serve a good end."[35]
Jordan knows that human malevolence and perspectival distortions
can render certain values dangerous. Even if the values of a Nazi
regime or the norms associated with apartheid are considered a
source of stability and continuity to the framers of those malignant
infrastructures, they fail Jordan's test. She requires that conviction
values enhance collective well-being and enhance the public good.
She also invites the reader/listener to participate in the discovery
of public values and to continue the process of constructing a reliable but resilient moral foundation. Because this process cannot
take place in a vacuum, Jordan challenges the nation to learn from
the past and to develop (or discover) relevant but consistent norms,
values, and sources of authority.

It is one thing to identify lofty moral ideals; it is quite another
to commend them as the norms and authorities that should inform the moral life. Although Jordan's norms educe foundational
precepts from complex moral, religious, legal, and philosophical
realms, the final formulation is set forth with simplicity. In a commencement speech given at Middlebury College, a year after her
"Conviction Values" speech, she returns to the same theme. This
time Jordan names the values she considers important or "common." However, it is clear that she works within the theoretical

framework that she identified in "Conviction Values." She invokes the same prima facie language. She says: "This is no time to debate whether to teach values, or the proper forum for such instruction. This is the time to identify those values we have in common and incorporate them into our rules for daily living."[36]

Accordingly, Jordan contends that some ideas are so basic to human flourishing that they should not be the subjects of controversy. In this speech entitled "Values in Common," Jordan describes the world that the students are about to enter. She says forthrightly that her generation has bequeathed nothing more than the debate over values rather than a settled legacy of moral rectitude.

Certainly, Jordan is aware that no generation ever accepts the values of another without struggle and protest. So, why does Jordan seem to prefer "settled moral values" over the vitality of debate when her moral theories rely upon public discourse and collective action? I am not certain that she does. Jordan is aware of her audience. She addresses the class of 1987, the children of the "hippie generation." They grew up with parents who tried to match their idealism with reality. Given the excesses of the decade, the violence, social disruptions, and the generational clashes, Jordan argues for common values as a continuing movement toward social harmony.

Jordan's four linchpins of moral endeavor are truth, toleration, respect, and community. These values are not exhaustive. However, they are prioritized, dynamic, and far less controversial than the issues that splintered society in the prior decade:

> I have not begun to exhaust the values we humans hold in common. What is the quality which makes and keeps these values as widely held and believed? Are they a matter of law, the violation of which is punished? Is there a great score-keeper in the sky waiting to call us in for a final accounting? If we don't keep these values, will we be blackballed from the neighborhood? The answer to each of these questions is No. We hold these values because they conform to the universal fitness of things. They are rational, natural, and conform to common sense.[37]

In this excerpt, Jordan reveals her source of authority for the norms and values that she commends. Although the languages of law, religion, and morality contribute to her moral formulations, they do not override the authority that she attributes to rationality and common sense. Jordan believes that truth is the first virtue of all human institutions. This is the virtue that must abide in all who purport to serve the public. Tolerance can be enacted passively but is the minimum requirement for those who expect to flourish in a diverse society. Respect is a logical extension of tolerance; it emerges as social beings make the transition from passivity to engaged moral sentiment. Each of the values that she identifies is within the reach and experience of ordinary people in their private lives. However, taken collectively they become the potential sites of moral transcendency.

Once norms are identified, Jordan wants them applied in the public sphere. Accordingly, she determines that politics is a primary forum for ethics. For Jordan, politics and ethics are not separable ideas. In fact, one of the more consistent themes in her speeches relates to ethics in government. She argues that ethics cannot be relegated to professional and personal spheres. Government must reflect the moral ideals of a virtuous citizenry. Jordan knows that the benefits of national values extend far beyond the political realm.

Keynote Addresses

On two important occasions, Jordan had an opportunity to present keynote addresses before Democratic conventions.[38] When she gave the keynote address in 1976, Jordan was the first black woman to address either political party. The speech was symbolic of dreams fulfilled. Jordan became not just another keynoter, but the embodiment of progress toward racial harmony and equality, irrespective of race or gender. Throughout the speech, Jordan's imposing presence is proof that some "dreams deferred" can be brought to fruition.[39]

Rhetoric scholar Wayne N. Thompson's analysis of this first keynote speech points out the difficulty of engaging two audiences: partisan delegates and silent television viewers. According to Thompson, Jordan's speech is successful because she mixes universal political claims with neutral but specific acknowledgments of party accomplishments.[40] I disagree. Although these skills are evident, they would not ensure the success of the speech.

Jordan's speech succeeds because she answers the practical question on everyone's mind. How do we win in November after decades of defeat? This is the only issue that requires a response. A good speech full of political truisms and sound bites would not suffice. Those avenues had been tried to no avail. Two years after Watergate, the nation views all politicians with suspicion. Jordan addresses those fears by refusing to conform to expectations. This would not be an ordinary address. Instead of politics, she offers values that potentially could set the "ship of state" back on course toward common goals.

In this speech, she defines both the future of the party and the future of the nation. These are her recommendations: (1) the development of a national community; (2) the return of governmental power to the people; (3) the use of governmental power to remove stumbling blocks to human flourishing: and (4) the enhancement of altruism through the replacement of radical individualism with common goals and personal fulfillment.[41] The values that she has so often commended reappear in this speech. Jordan touches upon controversial subjects but raises them in the context of the common good rather than special interests.[42]

In 1992, Jordan would give a second keynote address at the Democratic convention. This time the candidate was Bill Clinton, and the country had changed markedly. Liberalism and all that the term implies had become an anathema. The politics of difference prevailed, and the moral values that Jordan had espoused in her first keynote address seemed simplistic and out of reach. Could Jordan help the party reformulate an image more congruent with the new national self-image, and would she want to? Jordan was no longer in the public arena; she was a professor at the LBJ School, and she was disabled. Changes had occurred, and more changes would be needed if the Democrats were to win. Once again, as her wheelchair approached the podium, she embodied that change. Her speech was entitled "Change: From What to What?"[43]

Thematically, scene descriptions were central to her address. She was describing a political and moral landscape where change was invigorating and salutary. She concedes that the American dream, although not dead, is slipping away for the "have-nots." The scene of deprivation and poverty that Jordan describes is not unfamiliar. Over the years, the ranks of the deprived increased despite liberal social welfare projects. This unexpected result engendered a backlash from the dominant culture and nihilism among the marginalized.

Another change has occurred. One of her favorite themes, character ethics, has taken on a different nuance since the first allegations of Bill Clinton's womanizing have come to the attention of the nation. Jordan says: "Character has become an agenda item this political season. A well-reasoned examination of the question of character reveals more emotionalism than fact. It is reason and not passion which should guide our decisions."[44]

It isn't clear whether Jordan believes that Clinton embodies the moral values that she esteems. She does not live long enough to witness his impeachment proceedings or the Lewinsky shenanigans, but her rhetorical choices at the time of his nomination indicate an emphasis upon the scene rather than the agent or act. This choice allows her to shift her focus from direct considerations of the candidate's moral rectitude. In fact, she never mentions Bill Clinton's name in the body of her speech. She relies upon her familiar refrain "We the people." She does urge a change of the political milieu. This is a change that can occur through the will of the people.

This second keynote address is unusual because of Jordan's direct references to ethnicity. There are few national speeches where Jordan makes race/ethnicity central to her argument. In fact, unless she is making a speech specifically about race, she claims her identity and proceeds to deliver a speech that uses the language of equality in a neutral and universal way. But this speech is different. She proclaims the full equality of women and answers Rodney King's poignant question, "Can't we all get along?" with a resounding "yes!" This will be her last national political forum before her death in 1996. She concludes this speech with a profound statement and a poignant refrain. "We must profoundly change from the deleterious environment of the Eighties, characterized by greed, selfishness, mega-mergers, and debt overhang, to one characterized by devotion to the public interest and tolerance. And yes, love."[45]

As the applause reached a crescendo, Jordan could be heard repeating the mantra "LOVE...LOVE...LOVE!" Other commentators agree with Jordan's call for love. Michael Perry says:

> The imperative to "love one another as I have loved you" can be understood...not as a piece of divine legislation, but as a truly, fully human response to the question of how to live.... [Love] is the existential yield of a religious conviction about how the world (including we in the world) hangs together: in particular the conviction that the Other is finally one's own sister/brother — and should receive, therefore, the gift of one's loving concern.[46]

Jordan finally subsumes all of the variant lists of virtues and values into one word: love. Now, in the most unlikely place, a political rally, she uses her moral authority to speak in the language of public theology, commending love as the end of moral fulfillment, the ideal manifestation of the common good.

Envisioning the Common Good

> What happens to a dream deferred
> Does it dry up like a raisin in the sun?
> . . . .
> Maybe it just sags like a heavy load
> Or does it explode?
> — LANGSTON HUGHES[47]

One of the key themes in Jordan's speeches is "the common good." Jordan seeks those universal values that exemplify the highest ideals of human behavior and benefit the entire nation. Jordan's universalistic approach to human flourishing relies upon identifiable values. Like Oxford philosopher John Finnis, Jordan also contends that basic values are constitutive of human flourishing

and are ends rather than means.[48] They are intrinsically valuable.
However, Jordan's values are inextricably tied to the political process and public life. For Jordan, virtue and collective ends enhance
the potential of human flourishing in the private and public sphere.
But how can these determinations be made? Who should determine
which good should prevail? How should we resolve the dilemma
of incommensurate "goods" in a pluralistic culture? This section
discusses Jordan's conceptualization of the "common good" in an
era of the increasing privatization of desired human ends. The discussion begins with the conceptualization of human fulfillment in
Jordan's speeches. The second portion addresses the dilemma that
pluralism poses for the ideal construct. Finally, the section concludes with an inquiry as to whether secular and/or theological
foundations supply the premise upon which Jordan's values and
conceptualizations of the good are based.

Jordan assumes that certain moral dispositions are necessary
in order to desire good ends. In previous chapters, we have discussed the role that experience, family training, and habituation
play in the development of moral sensibilities. However commendable these processes are, Jordan recognizes that some people have
not been fortunate enough to have this upbringing. Moreover,
she is not naïve as to the difficulties of moral praxis in a world
where virtue and depravity are equally accessible human inclinations. Recognizing this fact, Jordan refers to the "common good"
as antithetical to human nature.[49]

Jordan believes that radical individualism destabilizes the impetus toward common goals. She wonders aloud whether the common good can compete against egocentrism writ large; whether
"a majority of the people in America society [can] be convinced
to make the changes necessary to pull all of our citizens into
a stream of hope and future and opportunity."[50] In this speech,
Jordan juxtaposes her consideration of the good against an en-
croaching corporate selfishness. Having been born in a Western
context, Jordan knows that the "good" is often synonymous with
private interests. Concomitantly, private interests are not only en-
sconced in the national mythology; they function as an incendiary
propellant to the competitive market forces that dominate American life. To understand how Jordan juggles the incongruities, it

is helpful to compare her discussion of the common good, in her keynote address of 1976, with her ideas of moral flourishing in speeches written two decades later.

In the earlier "Common Good" speech (1976), Jordan antic-ipates the argument that the common good and the American ideal are antithetical concepts. She knows that the culturally en-trenched myth of "rugged individualism" is inherent to the self-understanding of the majority culture. It also motivates American creativity and consumer lust. She also believes that the nation is better served by a reclamation of basic human goods. The task is to identify existing points of mutuality.

In her quest for mutuality, Jordan avoids immediate identifica-tion of the common good so that she can connect her theory with commonalities shared by a diverse citizenry. She begins with refer-ences to a common spirit, using the term in a secularized context, saying, "Are we to be one people bound together by a common spirit, sharing in common endeavor, or will we become a divided nation?"[51] The spirit to which Jordan refers emanates from the will of a people committed to a common national endeavor. She also alludes to the national community as the manifested out-come of that common spirit. However, there is a hindrance to that ideal. "But this is the danger America faces. That we will cease to become one nation and become instead a collection of inter-est groups, city against suburb, region against region, individual against individual — each seeking to satisfy private wants."[52]

Jordan depicts a worst case scenario of total chaos precipitated by a mutant form of radical individualism that becomes the an-tithesis of the liberty and public virtue envisioned by the founding fathers. For a generation weaned on assassination, street politics, and war, chaos is abhorrent. Jordan's litany of commonalities sug-gests an alternate path. She says, "A spirit of harmony will survive in America only if each one of us remembers that we share a common destiny."[53]

However, the path toward this goal is dimly lit because Jordan is not specific as to the actions, attitudes, and behaviors that will foster the communal well-being that she seeks. The fact that she uses broad rhetorical strokes when she refers to the common good contrasts with her detailed explication of moral characteristics and values. The difference in her approach may be attributed to a difference in purpose. Jordan's speeches on morality are instructive (offered for the purpose of education), whereas her speeches on the common good seek real consensus.

To achieve that consensus she asks the audience to participate in the process of defining commonalities. She says, "We must define the common good and begin again to shape a common good and a common future. Let each person do his or her part. If one citizen is unwilling to participate, all of us are going to suffer. For the American idea, though it is shared by all of us, is realized in each one of us."[54] Suddenly an abstract concept like "good" begins to take shape, and the dramaturgical meaning becomes tangible when expressed as the projected will of the people. This is the challenge that Jordan poses to a disillusioned generation poised to retreat from public life.

In 1990, Jordan again addresses the common good in response to a Ford Foundation report entitled *The Common Good, Social Welfare and the American Future.* The report addresses the social problems that divide the nation and offers specific funding solutions. Jordan commends the findings but once again cautions the reader/listener that "altruism is not a natural state. The preservation of self first is."[55] For Jordan, the solution to negative inclinations is concerted action and the habituation of will and endeavor to overcome the baser human instincts. She juxtaposes the solutions before Congress and the solutions outlined in the report and concludes that they are not significantly different. Her conclusions are simple but prescient. The common good can be inculcated into public policy, through (1) a revamping of the health-care system, (2) by addressing the blight of drug addiction, and (3) through education.[56]

Although Jordan is concerned about public policy issues, she also addresses the more controversial matter of ethnic pluralism that divides the country and hinders progress toward a unified community.

Moral Flourishing and Pluralism

Divisiveness/diversity—middle-class, underclass; homeowner, homeless; gay straight; the aged, the young. Whatever hap-

pened to E Pluribus Unum, from many one? Can we reinvig-
orate the American spirit and renew a sense of the common
good?[57]

In her later years, Jordan's flag-waving rhetoric becomes more
complex and attentive to dissenting voices. She is aware that
her depiction of America as a site of potential universal well-
being is flawed by historical reality. Ethnic groups seem more
polarized than ever, seeking isolation and exalting difference. Oppression and exploitation of marginalized groups have reached
levels of sophistication that far exceed the crude but devastating
manifestations of white supremacy during the 1950s and 1960s.

One thing is certain, Jordan does not have the luxury of for-
mulating a neutral theory of moral flourishing. For her vision of
the common good will not stand if she has not come to terms
with the dilemma of American's intransigent racism, xenophobia,
class inequities, and gender bias. Accordingly, Jordan concedes that
despite national rhetoric inclined toward common destiny, people
have been intentionally and viciously excluded from social and political processes. As a result, the moral fiber of the nation continues
to suffer irreparable harm.

It is in this section, devoted to an analysis of Jordan's ideas of
moral flourishing, that issues of exclusion become relevant. I have
discussed briefly the impact of her public emergence from a segregated society and her stance on issues of race. Now the issue
is whether Jordan can realistically formulate a viable theory of
human fulfillment on foundations of ethnic marginalization.

Jordan is a patriot who believes that the nation's greatness is
tested by its willingness to extend the American dream to all of
its citizens. In one of her later speeches she says: "Our strength is
rooted in our diversity. . . . But that diversity is rife with strain, tension, and doubt. A perfect union has not been formed." She goes
on to explain America's mission. She says: "It is to take its diversity
and mold it into a cohesive and coherent whole that would espouse virtues and values essential to the maintenance of civil order.
There is nothing easy about that mission. But it is not mission
impossible."[58]

Jordan's "E Pluribus Unum" speech is perhaps one of her more explicit speeches about the effect of diversity on the hope for moral flourishing. In the following excerpt, one sees the disjunctures between Jordan's lived experience and her moral vision. Although Jordan is committed to a concept of the common good, she cannot deny certain unpleasant realities. Something has happened to Jordan's tone and philosophy by the time she delivers the E Pluribus Unum speech. She places an emphasis upon patriotism, but her level of awareness of government involvement in human tragedy has increased markedly. In this speech, she catalogues the atrocities. This is tough talk for Jordan, as exemplified in the following excerpt worth quoting in full:

> We have our own history of ethnic cleansing carried out against the American Indians. Some of this was inadvertent through the transmission of white people's diseases during otherwise civil meetings to exchange or barter food and merchandise. But some of it was intentional genocide, through the deliberate transmission of diseases such as when pox was put in blankets given or sold to the Indians. One of the saddest chapters of our history was the Trail of Tears, the forced migration at the turn of the 19th century of the Cherokee Indians from their chosen homeland onto reservations picked for them by white men.[59]

Jordan is not attempting a precise accounting of the atrocities of one ethnic group against another. Rather, her remarks are intended to "acknowledge with regret" America's past and present sins. For Jordan, it is the least that moral responsibility requires of those who want to move toward the future. Moreover, she knows that the government is a convenient target for vilification, when in fact the racism, xenophobia, classism, and gender bias are deeply entrenched within the public consciousness. When she appeals to her audience to learn the lessons of history, she invites them to consider the connections between human action and human flourishing. She also implies that our best instincts are inevitably distorted when they are delegated and institutionalized without the vigilance of citizen oversight. Jordan considers citizen oversight necessary to forestall the emergence of new forms of oppression. In that regard, Jordan says:

The evidence is mounting about another form of deliberate disregard for the lives and health of minorities. I refer to what is called environmental racism: landfills, sewage plants, toxic waste incinerators, and other sources of toxic pollution that tend to be located in low income and minority areas. This environmental racism creates another loop of the cycle of poverty.... The roots of environmental racism often go deep into the histories of zoning codes, and the inability of those codes to keep up with growing populations.... Environmental racism is new.[60]

This speech excerpt evinces an inescapable sense of the relentlessness of human depravity. Rhetorically, Jordan juxtaposes opposite possibilities to evoke thought. The listener must consider the implications of actions that are deeply rooted in history but only recently have come to public attention. Environmental racism may be new, but the roots are deep. This is an acknowledgment that political and legal solutions may never reach or solve the crux of civic problems. Moreover, problems are increasing rather than decreasing, as the cultural base becomes more diverse with the influx of new immigrants.

One wonders how Jordan's speeches can contemplate a consensus about the common good in an environment where new participants in the sociopolitical project do not share the same language or symbolic and mythic assumptions about the path toward moral fulfillment. According to theologian William Dean, one such myth is that "beneath the variety of American meanings there was a core of meaning: that America had received an extraordinary blessing, one that set her apart from other nations."[61] This mythic understanding reached a pinnacle in the theory of exceptionalism. Exceptionalism depicts the United States as God's new Israel. Sociologist Robert Bellah agrees with Dean that the concept of God and morality was so embedded in the national consciousness that any loss or revision of the narrative would prove to be damaging to public policy, the participation and the spirit of the people.[62]

Jordan sets up a scenario where the basic elements of a democratic society are not only abstract principles; they are also mediating social factors amenable to the reconstructive influences of public dialogue. Public discourse is seen as the necessary precursor to moral performance. Moreover, she contends that "democratic pluralism requires an agreement to be locked in public argument over disagreements of consequence within the bonds of civility."[63] She continues: "If we have differences so deep and profound that they threaten public order and civility, they should be brought out into the open, discussed and debated, and if possible, resolved. If resolution is not possible every effort should be made to reach a consensus through compromise."[64] Jordan believes that a well-ordered society cannot respond to internal conflicts unless public discourse is a viable option. She also knows that a difficult conversation about ethnicity is needed to challenge the belief that every "us" requires a "them." This is language that inevitably fans the flames of xenophobia.[65]

In earlier speeches, Jordan postulates the problematic Americanization ethic as a solution to immigration issues. This theory is a conception of the common good that assumes a homogeneity of national and cultural interests. It is the theory most often associated with the "melting pot" theme. This metaphor assumes a mold of conformity that dissolves cultural and ethnic particularities.[66]

According to the melting pot theory, the only true Americans reflected the image of the white Protestant majority. In order to achieve consensus as to the collective interests of the nation in a diverse population, this "melt down" ideal had to be instilled in the national consciousness. In this regard, appropriations of Israel Zangwill's play helped to sear the image of American homogeneity into the minds of the citizenry. Some versions of Zangwill's play depicted foreigners dressed in ethnic costumes, stepping into a huge pot and emerging as well-dressed, accent-free Americans.[67] Current Americanization initiatives can be discerned in the argument for "English only." Such theories rid America of its ethnic minorities by ridding minorities of their ethnicity. Americanization requires submission to a powerful hegemony. This is a depiction of the common good that is disquieting and untenable.

As Chair of the U.S. Commission on Immigration Reform, Jordan had the opportunity to clarify her ideas about public policy issues, diversity, and the common good. Jordan says this about Americanization: "That word earned a bad reputation when it was used by racists and xenophobes in the 1920s. The commission believes we must revitalize the concept as the best way to ensure a continuing tradition of generous immigration polices. Americanization policies should help newcomers learn to speak, read, and write English effectively. They should strengthen civic understanding in the teaching of American history for all Americans. And, they should encourage all Americans to fulfill their civic responsibilities."[68]

Moreover, Jordan and her colleagues on the Immigration Commission concluded that the following three premises should guide further revisions of immigration policy: (1) immigration is in the national interest as long as it comports with the goals and regulations of the United States; (2) illegal immigration serves no national interest and must be curbed; (3) immigration is more than admittance. Finally, the Commission determined that successful immigration requires an integrative Americanization process.

Jordan's conservatism and philosophical retreat from the liberal political agenda are most evident in her attempt to reconcile the interests of immigrants with her notions of the common good. Although details of her service on the Immigration Commission are beyond the scope of this inquiry, her theories regarding the inclusion of refugees and immigrants are relevant to her theories of the national community and the common good.

Jordan begins with the premise that the United States is a nation of immigrants. However, not enough is said about the fact that the first wave of immigrants occupied an already occupied land and then required subsequent immigrants to emulate, imitate, and reflect their image. As a consequence, inherited social policies approach difference as an incommensurable foreignness rather than otherness or the separateness of reconcilable parts of a whole.[69]

Although her intentions seem to be good, Jordan's rhetoric about immigration is infused with the myopic fears of the majority culture. She might have avoided this pitfall if she had distinguished the common good from majority interests in maintaining the status quo. Or she might have invited her listeners to take a closer look at the inequities of U.S. immigration policies that favored European immigrants over refugees from Third World countries. Another option would have been to apply the same rhetorical strategies that she used during the Watergate hearings and allow the leading characters to expose their hidden motives.

Without the benefit of these insights, one can consider Jordan's recommendations as only the beginning of a public conversation that must be reconvened. This is not to say that her recommendations are not viable as theoretical possibilities. It is to say that absorption and integration in the form of Americanization may not be the catalysts for moral flourishing in a multiethnic society.

Jordan's position on immigration and a required national registry drew much criticism. In response, Jordan said: "The United States needs a national ID card, and it's not going to bring the Gestapo into your bedroom."[70] Here Jordan misses the point. There are certain initiatives that might fulfill legal mandates but offend the human spirit. In the words of Abraham Heschel: "If a [person] is not more than human, [that person] is less than human."[71] The nation's leaders are therefore charged with a mandate to offer the best opportunities for persons to be fully human.

One wonders whether a restrictive national registry program for immigrants satisfies that mandate. The answer to that question depends on whether immigrants are perceived as a threat to the national economy, or whether they present an opportunity to encounter God in the personhood of difference? To be certain, moral considerations of immigration goals require a shift from paternalism to relationality. Such shifts seldom occur without the impetus of public dialogue.

Theorist Dana Wilbanks characterizes the work of ethics in situations like immigration and aid to refugees. She says: "Ethics is not primarily the construction of a rational framework of thought about moral matters. Rather it is a vision of life in relation to God that is to be embodied historically in a community. The ethic is to be lived, not just refined, clarified, and talked about."[72] For good or ill, the common good is deeply textured with the nuances of individual desires and dreams. Jordan believes that the authentic act of Americanization is the ability of this nation to contain and nurture difference. She suggests that moral proclivities are honed into deliberative discernments when they encounter conflicting and resonating values in the public sphere. She also considers the quest for common values to be of primary public concern — too important, in fact, to become the specialty of any one domain.

In retrospect, her efforts to apply her theories of the common good in a practical setting (immigration) seem to be impeded by the constraints of politics, changing economic realities, and her own conservative view of what citizenship entails. For Jordan, the issue of immigration was, in fact, a forum to begin this process. She was confident that the common good would become apparent in the midst of contested values. The question that remains unanswered is whether that good could be articulated in more than one language, and whether the nation would be willing to envision a thick, copious, and culturally dynamic model.

Jordan dies before she can complete a public discussion that might have contributed to a change in her position. One thing is certain: She does not hesitate to voice her views, popular or not. She urges those who disagree with her position to bring their ideas into the public sphere to confront, contend, and compromise with others.

I began this chapter with a passage from an article entitled "Here Be Dragons." Baldwin ends this article with a statement that is relevant for this conclusion. Baldwin says: "We are part of each other. Many of my countrymen [and women] appear to find this fact exceedingly inconvenient and even unfair, and so, very often, do I. But none of us can do anything about it."[73] Jordan believes that something can be done about this inescapable relationality: the nation can engage in moral discourse and value identification intended to demarcate and solidify a basis for unity.

The next chapter moves the discussion from moral theory to public religion. Jordan's speeches on this subject combine her pragmatic inclinations and commonsense rhetoric with a recognition that religious language is too important to the amelioration of difference in the public sphere to limit its scope to faith communities. In this respect, Jordan says: "I enlist a winning coalition to drive the American Dream to an inexorable and glorious conclusion. The pillars I enlist are the government, business, and the Church."[74] She has chosen unlikely partners; on this, the dreamers of every ilk and origin agree. But for Jordan, these cross alliances are necessary; the dreams have been deferred long enough.

Chapter 5

Religion in the Public Sphere: What of the Night?

Which voice will influence — the voice of those who seek peace and justice and the establishment of Christian love, or will the dominant voice be that of the gun and sword, which constantly seeks to destroy, and terrorize, and subject.

— BARBARA JORDAN[1]

This is a time to cry out.... We have imprisoned God in our temples and slogans, and now the word of God is dying on our lips. There is darkness in the East, and smugness in the West. What of the night? What of the night?

— RABBI ABRAHAM JOSHUA HESCHEL[2]

Barbara Jordan and Rabbi Heschel consider the human voice a creative and evocative tool capable of correcting the image of religion as a pietistic exile from the world. The thought is provocative. If the Word of God is imprisoned in the religious sphere, it dies on the lips of its wardens. What of the night? It can be a reasonable and welcome alternative to the heat of the day, if the discourse of the world, the church, the synagogue, and the mosque intersect at dawn or eventide.[3]

Jordan's religious speeches are a great find. They include her addresses to a wide variety of religious organizations, and connect her moral and constitutional theories to a heartfelt faith. In the speeches, her faith transcends personal witness to become public discourse about the issues that affect the life of the national community. In this chapter Jordan's use of religious language and symbolism is considered with the religious perspectives of Abraham Heschel, Malcolm X, and Rudolf Otto. The first section begins with a brief summary of Jordan's traditional religious background and concludes with a discussion of public religion, public theology, and secularization. The second section probes Jordan's view of responsibility and faith. The chapter ends with a discussion of the constructive role that public theology plays in Jordan's formulation of a "more perfect union."

When Jordan uses the term religion, she is referring to sacred elements that pervade daily life and provide the elements necessary for wholeness and well-being. She believes that public religion and politics are necessary partners in the effort to sustain a free society. She says: "When I decided to go into politics, I had a very long conversation with Christ, and wondered whether it would be possible in the public arena, which is supposed to be divorced from things religious and spiritual, to perform in a political capacity and remain true to my Christian heritage."[4] She decides that she can.

Jordan's premise is that there is an inherent mutuality between religion and culture, and that there are no radical disjunctures between the sacred and the secular, the political and the moral. Each sphere impinges upon and contributes to the flourishing or decline of the other. In this regard, Abraham Heschel makes a statement that is profoundly congruent. He observes that "the road to the sacred leads to the secular."[5] An astute observer might add that the opposite is also true because the world is a whole — one complexly interwoven piece.

"Train Up a Child in the Way She Should Go..."

Jordan's religious upbringing is well documented. Her father was a Baptist minister, and her mother was an orator in the church. Jordan began speaking publicly at an early age in the Good Hope Missionary Baptist Church. In fact, her life was so enmeshed with the church that while she was at Boston University she considered changing her major from law to religion so that she might enter the ministry. Howard Thurman was the chaplain who made such a profound impression on her.

Jordan remembers that while she was under the watchful care of her father and paternal grandfather, religion seemed to focus on all of the things that could not and should not be done. It wasn't until she was in Boston that she felt free to make her own choices. It was only then that she told herself, "You know you don't have to go to church if you don't want to. But then I found that I wanted to. I wanted to go to chapel, and I went practically every Sunday."[6] Of Thurman's special appeal, she adds that his speeches differed from the messages that she was familiar with at Good Hope because Thurman focused on the nexus between faith and the practical matters of everyday life. She loved his realism and his use of language and enthusiastically "repreached" his sermons to her roommates.[7]

For a while it looked as if she was headed toward the ministry. When Jordan announced this possible life direction, her father was elated and told her that as a "missionary" she would be following in the footsteps of his mother, Mary Jordan. This was not what Jordan intended. Her vision of ministry included women in the pulpit and in positions of authority equal to men. Her father's reaction gave her pause. The church might be the site of potential spiritual transformation, but its responses to gender issues were as limited as the wider community. For many contributing reasons, including Jordan's love of the law, she continues to nurture her spiritual life in Thurman's chapel services but focuses on law rather than ministry as a career.

As the speeches reveal, this was not really an either/or choice for Jordan, as her religious sensibilities were an integral part of her personal and professional development. Interestingly enough, her religious views are simplistic and unexamined in contrast to the debates that swirl around her. While she is making her religious speeches, the black theology movement (James Cone, William R. Jones, and others) depicts the Christian faith as the vanguard flank of a social revolution. J. Deotis Roberts and other traditionalists suggest that black liberation theology may be more political than religious, and Malcolm X and other black nationalists urge a wholesale defection from Christianity.[8]

Into this context, Jordan brings her own "Sunday school" faith to the discourse and welcomes the challenge of other voices. In this way, she models the immediacy and accessibility of a public discourse that does not require the advanced credentials or critique of professionals. It is a practice that can be engaged even at basic levels of faith and understanding.

Jordan's spirituality is motivated as much by concerns for the general welfare of the community and public service as it is by the mysteries of faith. In addition to the unfathomable aspects of God's interiority, Jordan also understands God as an accessible and generative source of all commendable human endeavors — an entity simultaneously immediate and distant, loving but capable of wrath, sought after but possessing inherently dangerous powers that discourage frivolity. Holy Scripture invokes many instances that support this view. Moses' face glowed during an encounter with God.[9] Uzziah died when he touched the Ark of the Covenant.[10] From a human point of view, cautious covenant would seem to be a reasonable guideline for relationships with this powerful God. Yet Jordan proposes a working mutuality that recognizes and respects the differences between the created and the Creator. She argues that all matters are complete in the God who operates beyond human control but is also "a worker in human history. The operative word is *in*. God is not peripheral to history."[11] For Jordan, the very fact that God is an integral part of human history makes human relationships possible.

In her religious speeches, God is not depicted as "wholly other" but as an accessible conversation partner familiar with (if not the originator of) pragmatic concerns. Malcolm X recounts a similar dialogical relationship with the Almighty, but one that is unique to his own religious perspectives. He says: "When I was the personification of evil.... I would force myself back down into the praying-to-Allah posture. When finally I was able to make myself stay down — I didn't know what to say to Allah."[12] Jordan considers an ongoing conversation with God a human legacy and right. Malcolm is silenced by his own perceived inadequacy and human failings. Yet both persist in translating their own faith languages into the political arena. In Malcolm's case, bell hooks says: "Clearly he desired there to be a perfect harmony between that worship and the political efforts of the Nation [of Islam] to decolonize black minds."[13] Jordan sees the fate of African Americans and other minorities as inextricably connected to the sociopolitical interests of the nation. Malcolm is not certain, even after his pilgrimage to Mecca, that integration at any level can benefit minorities. However, God is an integral part of both quests for the resolution of political and social problems.

Jordan's speeches also address the role of the Holy Spirit as "the comforter" and active renewer of faith and openness within each person:

> The Holy Spirit is active in us. It continually renews our faith and our beliefs; as we confront the complexities of the world, we desperately need this constant renewal to strengthen us and show us how to respond to the great challenges of being a believer. It is this renewal of, and opening up by, the Holy Spirit within us that is our defense against dogmatism.[14]

This potential for renewal inspires the ultimate hope of communal reconciliation. Because this hope is divinely inspired, it is not compromised by the human penchant toward intransigence and evil. Jordan welcomes the openness that the Holy Spirit engenders as a necessary precursor to common goals. Most public orators would shy away from such blatantly faith-based discourse. Jordan does not. She is a skilled translator of religious language into public rhetoric; she makes her references to God and the Holy Spirit concrete and applicable in daily life without eliminating their inherent "otherness." She also recognizes that whenever humanity translates the "holy" into intellectually accessible categories, there is always something left over that cannot be totally subsumed. This remainder is "beyond the sphere of the usual, the intelligible and the familiar."[15] Like philosopher Rudolf Otto, she seems to be aware that although reason and order can be an aspect of the sacred, the absolute rationalization of religion rolls the religious experience out so thin and flat as to eliminate it altogether.[16] Jordan and Otto both conclude that the meaning of holiness, or "the numinous," far exceeds the limits of human conceptual categories.

Jordan makes no attempt to reconcile the mysteries of faith with public preferences for objectivity. She approaches the "sacred" in both a subjective and objective sense. The following example clarifies this distinction:

Imagine someone saying to a Bosnian Serb: "The Bosnian Muslim, too, no less than you is sacred.... It is wrong for you to rape her." If sacred is meant in the subjective sense, the Bosnian Serb may reply, "sacred to you and yours perhaps but not to me." By contrast, sacredness in the objective sense implies that the violation of another human being transcends any personal code of values; it violates the very order of creation.[17]

By contrast, Jordan merges her subjective discernments about the sacred with objective proposals for the moral well-being of the wider community. She has no patience with those who use private definitions of the sacred realm to abuse others.

Thus far, I have discussed the role that the Holy Spirit and God play in Jordan's speeches. Both are completely spiritual entities mediated through human interpretive processes. Jesus is another question entirely. Embodied as totally human and totally divine, the question arises as to how this second person of the Godhead can fulfill the same function as God and the Holy Spirit in public religious discourse. In other words, can Jesus be interjected into a religiously diverse public arena apart from fundamentalism, dogmatism, or evangelism?

Few would disagree that where the "isms" prevail, there is little likelihood of mutuality. Jordan offers another option. When Jesus is considered the inquisitor and conversant partner of humankind, the isms retreat. Jordan says that as she grew up she made the transition from "seeing Christ in the abstract, to being able to communicate on a one-to-one basis."[18] She often speaks of the conversational relationship that she has with Christ and the importance of that ongoing dialogue in her life. She says: "My father was a Baptist minister, and Church, Christ, God, religion were always important in our family.... [S]o how important was and is Christianity in my life? It provides for me the reason for being me." She goes on to say, "I cannot live my life not loving the people who surround me and call myself a Christian."[19] Jordan's religious sensibilities constitute a focalizing belief system for her philosophical and political views; they are also a motivating impetus for her attempts to enact kingdom principles pragmatically.

The principles that Jordan espouses begin with Christian precepts of love expressed in the care and support of other human beings. Next, these imperatives are translated into mandates for a life of public service. In essence, she suggests a theory of human existence that runs contrary to the prevailing materialistic individualism of the age. Jordan contends that we enter an ongoing social world for the purpose of enhancing the life of the human community. Because that community is diverse by definition, our contributions must be drawn from multiple sources including religion.

Mediating the Discourses of Church and State

Religion can be a constructive or destructive component in public life. Jordan's decision to include religion in her moral and political discourse resists the liberal trend that attempts to relegate religion to the private realm. When Jordan conjoins the languages of ethics, public religion, and jurisprudence, she proposes a synthesis that has been ostensibly lost. A strange interplay of fear and disdain contributed to the decline of public religious discourse in the United States. On the one hand, an increasingly liberal and secular culture lost confidence in the claims of religious communities, regarding with skepticism their ability to ameliorate increasingly complicated social issues. On the other hand, there was an overriding interest in protecting the republic from the abuses of religious zealots. The result was that religion was expelled from the public sphere.

Resistance to religious involvement in matters of public policy and politics in North America usually centers around the following themes: the real or imagined transgression of civil boundaries; the specter of an oppressive religiosity that might seek "purity" as a primary goal; and the threat to religious freedom.[20] Jordan refuses to widen the breach between the communities that nurture and inform our moral development and the joint civic project launched by the founders of the nation. Instead, she argues for a dialogical interrelationship that respects constitutional separations but recognizes the historical linkages between faith and culture.

In a speech to the National Religious Liberty Conference in

Washington, D.C., she traces the national discomfort with issues of church and state to Mark 12:17. About this scripture, Jordan says:

> Jesus said in response to a question designed to trick him "then render unto Caesar the things that are Caesar's and to God the things that are God's." Almost two thousand years since he said that, we have trouble figuring out what is Caesar's and what is God's. That ambivalence may underlie the reluctance of some to endorse the involvement of the church in public policy.[21]

Although Jordan affirms the separation of church and state as a valid constitutional principle, she contends that the metaphors and figures of speech contained therein have been twisted into a rule of law. An unintended wall has been erected between the "garden of the church" and the "wilderness of the world."[22] Jordan admits that the amendment to the Constitution that guarantees religious liberty is veiled in obscurity. However, she adds in a mischievous way that "history is not helped by preachers running for President."[23] Clearly, Jordan has her own ideas about where walls of separation might be useful. Jordan is convinced that the dialogue about church/state relations is artificial and a hindrance to the common good. Her concerns focus upon the isolation of communities of faith from public discourse about the common good. Under such circumstances, the church becomes something that it was never intended to be — a secluded spiritual enclave. According to Jordan, ecclesial bodies should be integral partners in America's social experiment:

> As a country we have not been uncomfortable invoking the name of God in our undertakings. We have recognized that as a matter of common sense there is a power larger and greater than we are. That consensus recognition does not alter the relationship of the church and the state. There is no hostility in that relationship except on the part of the atheist.... The church is the institution that helps us move God from the theoretical, the abstract to the real, the concrete. The church and the state often meet in their common field of action, [hu]man[kind].[24]

Jordan realizes that the God of history exceeds human evaluative categories. Consequently, any movement from theoretical
and abstract to concrete occurs within the limitations of human
conceptualization and does not diminish the incalculable transcendence of God. However, transcendence does not hold center stage
in this speech; rather, the operative word, the one that works hard-
est for Jordan, is "common sense." If faith is a matter of common
sense, then the task of orienting faith communities toward new
responsibilities becomes less daunting. An appeal to reason and
common sense could accomplish that end. Common sense becomes
an interlocutor and facilitator of a more inclusive public sphere.
Jordan describes the human faculty of common sense as unfettered
and free — free to believe in the unseen God and to discern the
differences between constitutional protections and constitutional
misinterpretations.

When Jordan discusses issues of church and state, she confronts
the nation's extreme and sometimes irrational sensitivities about
the subject. Given the seriousness of these pervasive concerns, definition and clarity become crucial to the reassertion of religious
rhetoric into public discourse. A close analysis of the speeches reveals that Jordan's use of religious rhetoric conjoins the discourse
of public religion, public theology, and secularization. At this point
in the discussion, definitions of relevant terms would be helpful.

Public religion is not a description of television evangelism.
Rather, it is "a function of brand-name religion. It refers to the way
in which a specific religious tradition or community appropriates its
distinctive resources to contribute to the upbuilding of community
life."[25] The phrase "public religion" emphasizes the movement of religious language from private to public spheres. "Public theology" as
reflective practice "signifies the embrace of a public form of religious
argumentation."[26] It also encourages the reflexive considerations of
a reordered society toward broader philosophical and religiomoral
considerations of what is good and what is common. This practice
will be discussed in more depth at the end of the chapter.

The third concept, "secularization," is the most problematic for
those who define the term in ways that are oppositional to faith.
Given Jordan's Baptist upbringing and openly articulated religious
convictions, some explanation is necessary as to the role that secu-

larization plays in her speeches. Catholic theologian José Casanova gives a helpful account of secularization conceived in three distinctive ways: as displacement, as decline, and as a process of communication.[27] The displacement/decline theories allude to the central role that religion once held as an organizing principle for all other spheres of human activity. This theory assumes that the ascendancy of democratic sociopolitical theory displaces religion's centrality in society.

Jordan doesn't ascribe to a theory of secularization as displacement or decline, for her language does not contemplate a radical breach between spheres of influence. Instead, the sacred and the secular merge in the public arena. As communication, secularization is the process whereby certain ideas are translated and converge as they flow fluidly from disparate sources that contribute to public policy.

Jordan takes an interesting approach to Christian involvement in public policy issues. She seeks a balance of reason and faith that may be problematic in a Christian context for balance is not the singular core of Christianity. Radical obedience, risk taking, and challenges to the social order are values that have primacy in Holy Scripture. Jordan is not an advocate of radical solutions. Her approach to issues of public policy and faith reflect her own political and religious conservatism. This conservatism is perpetually challenged by her need for justice and the liberal transformation of society. This disparity between the desire for balance and the mandate for radical challenges to the existing order is unresolved in her rhetoric.

Jordan's use of religious language comports with her view that our daily lives are infused with a reality that is simultaneously political and transcendent. When I speak of transcendence in this context, I refer to Jordan's belief that operative faith in secular contexts can bridge sociopolitical divisions. The ultimate goal is the restoration of common goals and shared values. The clearest utilization of these rhetorical bridges occurs in Jordan's religious speeches. A key example is found in her statement about politics and faith. Here Jordan says, "Politics doesn't represent a divorcement from Christianity, but it represented a different kind of opportunity to actualize Christianity."[28] Jordan describes Christianity as a "springboard" for her public service. Her commitment is clear: "I consider myself not as one of those who would use Christianity as a political tool to defeat one's enemies and promote one's friends, but to use Christianity in politics to help one's friends and enemies. There is no base as universal as a Christian base."[29]

In this excerpt, Jordan identifies with her audience through the use of familiar language but expands the meaning of commonplace terms. Christianity in secular guise no longer divides society on the basis of confessional attestations but becomes a facilitator of unity in the wider community. Jordan depicts Christianity as a mediator of moral and political conflicts. This is a view of Christianity that exceeds private faith experiences to become a "universal base," a translatable language understood and efficacious beyond an immediate faith community.

Some might take exception to Jordan's final statement that "there is no base as universal as a Christian base." However, it is clear that this statement does not stake out "pietistic turf." Rather, this concluding sentence invites other faith communities to make similar claims. Although Jordan's faith context is unquestionably Christian, the statement can withstand the substitution of Islam, Buddhism, Judaism, and others. Jordan encourages faith communities to extract common claims or core beliefs from their own religious context that will enhance public life. One can imagine a scenario where divergent religions publicly dialogue in ways that educate and facilitate shared information. This has happened to some extent with the recent Western fascination with indigenous culture and ritual, but not in any purposeful or integrative way.

However, Jordan neither romanticizes the complex task of harmonizing disparate religious languages nor eliminates the possibility of conflict as a potential outcome of this effort. Instead, she asserts that religious claims, whether congruent or not, contribute to the moral and political ends of the nation. Moreover, Jordan insists that the nation's founders anticipated the warrant for religious participation in the formation of a flourishing national community. The following important excerpt emphasizes this point:

> The areas of morality and moral judgments are not the exclusive province and automatic arena of Christian con-

cern, just as the political process is not the private property
of the politician. The field of action in both concerns is
[hu]man[kind]. . . . The Christian must not abdicate [the] right
to affect and influence those vital structures. [They] must
become a partner with the politician and statesmen in the
process of structuring and restructuring . . . life. . . . The Christian must become an involved partner, and his [or her] faith
must accompany . . . and help release him [or her].[30]

In this early speech, entitled "The Role and Concern of Christian Women in Politics," Jordan argues that the partnership of
politics and religion may avert future social disasters. She says,
"Today, our very survival depends upon the decisions of our
political leadership."[31] Her conclusion is more prophetic than
apocalyptic, for she projects the outcome of discernible cultural
trends. Ultimately, she concludes that trends toward dehumaniza-
tion and decadence cannot contribute to the common good. Jordan
also contends that it should be possible for all religions to agree
that what is good for human beings is also what makes them
more human.

For Jordan, dialogue precedes decision-making. She knows that
despite the paranoia that continues to surround the subject of
religion and politics, both are firmly entrenched in the public
sphere. She realizes that divisions between the two are sedimented
remnants of sectarian strife, the legacy of political and ecclesial
struggles for power in pre-Enlightenment Europe.[32] What remains
in Jordan's era are conceptual divisions that do not match her
cultural memory.

Jordan remembers a community of believers for whom prayer
was sometimes the only option. But can prayer be included as a
viable discourse in public contexts? A prayer that Jordan gave during a national prayer breakfast provides intriguing insights into her
understanding of prayer as a viable public discourse. The prayer
falls within the ambit of public speech because it is offered as a
public rather than private entreaty. Jordan begins with supplication
and statements about human inadequacy without God. A litany
of "abilities" follows, in which she establishes the "we can't/God
can" dichotomy.

The language is not unusual until Jordan reaches the plea. She says, "Since You can do all that we cannot do, give us the good sense to work with you in partnership for the benefit of all humankind. Help us to resist our inclination to be the senior partner. As we work together, keep talking to us and help us to listen."[33] Once again the language of divine/human partnership surfaces. Here she refers to the joint action of humankind and God. Although the idea of partnership is not unusual in the Christian tradition, the language is usually muted.

Interestingly enough, Jordan prays that God will "move so powerfully within us that we shall be able to avert sinfulness."[34] This request seems to alter the nature of the partnership that she originally seeks. The entire prayer maintains this tenuous balance between a desire for mutuality and the awesome implication of partnership with holiness. Neither does Jordan resolve the anomaly that seems to arise whenever the language of divine intervention is used in conjunction with the languages of reason and human intellect. She says: "Common sense tells us that good citizenship and church membership are not mutually exclusive.... What is required are men and women of good will, willing to bargain in good faith for the common good. Reason must be their guide."[35] In this speech, Jordan assumes that reason and intellect are instilled in humankind through the activities of a reasoning God. If that is the case, then faith and reason are not contradictory ideas.

Responsibility and Faith

Barbara Jordan poses crucial questions in her religious speeches about the roles and responsibilities of Christians and the church in a democratic society. Inherent in the questions is the assumption that both must secure "the proper balance of elements needed for all individuals to pursue the fulfillment of body, mind and spirit."[36] For Jordan, this fulfillment occurs when faith and responsibility are active components of daily life. When Jordan talks about faith she refers to human/divine ties. But she also suggests that faith is manifested as the human impetus to act responsibly in the world.

Jordan's views on individual responsibility are presented in a speech given at the Silver Anniversary Women's Day celebration at Good Hope Missionary Baptist Church.[37] In this speech entitled "Women in Action: Religious, Responsible Role Models," Jordan's remarks evoke the image of the "virtuous woman" spoken of in Proverbs 31:25–30. Here the virtuous woman stars as an example of civic responsibility. Jordan begins by delineating her primary responsibilities:

> A myriad of disruptions cry out for the presence of a woman of virtue to re-establish the preeminence of the family as society's primary teacher of values and ethics. The family usually develops a core sense of values in cooperation and conjunction with the church.... The family comes armed with right and righteousness, honor and truth, justice and fairness and a commitment to Christ and his teachings.[38]

This secular interpretation of the virtuous woman emphasizes her role as a regenerator of families and a teacher of moral sensibilities. Cast against a litany of societal woes, her positive attributes become even more pronounced. Jordan is aware of the sociopolitical myths of "true womanhood" that contrast with myths about African American women. She was the victim of those perverse characterizations of black women as mammy, Sapphire, and Aunt Jemima. In contrast, Jordan puts the spotlight on this biblical model of womanhood, while maintaining a subliminal backdrop of uncomfortable facts and statistics about the black community.

In this speech, Jordan also recounts the alarming statistics that nearly 50 percent of black children are being raised in poverty, and 60 percent are born to single women. She says, "What does that tell us about their prospects for the future — their hopes and dreams?"[39] Jordan's question details the failures of the wider society and the increasingly fragile infrastructure of the African American community. The question that is implied but unspoken is whether the mantle of responsibility to self and community will be shouldered by this generation.

Jordan addresses two audiences: older black women who reinvented themselves in the image of the majority culture to little or no avail; and she addresses younger women in the church who have rejected the remaining choices — assimilation or alienation.

Jordan delivers a hard message to both in the guise of a pep talk. Her point is that churchwomen have not escaped the social maladies of the 1990s. She is warning them that the angel of death is loose, claiming the offspring of the faithful with the same regularity as those beyond hallowed grounds.

These are the sobering statistics: "Murder is now the leading cause of death among black males ages 15 through 24. Whatever happened to respect for human life and the unequivocal commandment 'Thou shalt not kill'?" She continues, "God values each life. We are his creatures.... How dare us devalue such a creation as God's gift of life! We cannot tolerate murder as the premier cause of destabilization and elimination of black life."[40] The rising death toll is so appalling that one wonders whether someone has forgotten to mark the doorposts with the blood of the lamb, or whether God is requiring more of "latter day saints." The unspoken challenge of these dire predictions of community dissolution is to the black church.

Jordan loves the black church for its role in sustaining a community under siege, but recognizes its limitations. Most commentators recognize the positive role that the black church has maintained in the African American community as an economically independent organization, the facilitator of civil rights, and the nurturer of black leadership. Within its safety, blacks performed and observed enactments of spiritual and moral goals. Moreover, the church served as a "staging area" for secular ventures.

However, another irrefutable (though less recognized) aspect of black religion has been its tendency to resolve critical tensions cathartically and eschatologically rather than pragmatically. Booker T. Washington derided "ignorant and immoral preachers," concluding that the manifest sign of racial progress was the trend toward secular rather than ministerial careers.[41] W. E. B. Du Bois "blamed the deep fatalism of the emancipated" on the message of the church.[42] James Baldwin inferred that religious ceremonies merged the languages of passion plays and minstrel shows to offer the community a sanitized view of race relations.[43] The complaints of Joseph R. Washington and Benjamin Mays seem to focus on the mystical/magical and religiodramatic themes prevalent in most churches.[44] This is a state of affairs that they deemed not to be in the best interests of the black community. Even the Black Liberation movement tried to distance itself from religious mysticism by emphasizing a radically politicized interpretation of Christian doctrine.

It is interesting to note that the charges against the black church are similar to those lodged against Victor Turner's theory of liminality. Turner's critics charge that ritual antistructure cathartically deflects organized opposition to oppressive social structures. Where the church is concerned, critics contend that an otherworldly emphasis also delays and channels social protest. Both arguments fail to probe deeply enough. Critics of Turner's theory fail to note that expressions of resistance in indigenous cultures do not necessarily follow Western expectations. In fact, ritual antistructure provides a format as well as the implicit authority to resist oppressive cultural institutions. Likewise, the church stands astride intersecting realms and, potentially, can balance the impetus for immediate social reform with the expectation of God's coming reign.

Jordan plainly states her specific issues with the black church, but then shifts to a wider context. She is aware that the church universal has several diseased extremities: the uncritical acceptance of the hierarchical, materialistic, and aberrant behaviors of society; the desire to conform ecclesial moral imperatives to popular standards; a retreat from public discourse; the mimicking of capitalistic initiatives; and an apparent inability to salvage a disintegrating public life. The church is complicit in the Western obsession with consumerism, and the resultant economic villainy erodes the possibility of human flourishing.

When Jordan challenges the church, she evokes the spirit and rhetoric of one of her spiritual mentors, Howard Thurman. She says: "We concentrate on becoming the nation which excels in economic growth, in military might, in conquering outer space. This concentration works to the detriment of [our] "inner space," and the development of [our] creativity and inner sources."[45] She concludes that this competitiveness and the obsession with "outdoing" the world have unraveled the more important concern for individual needs and joint responsibilities.

Jordan is aware that the failure to act responsibly is as prevalent in the church as it is in the secular community. However, she expects the church to use its transcendent and political potential to mediate such problems successfully. If, as she suspects, responsibility as a virtue or value has eluded an entire generation, it will not be reclaimed at this late date unless the choices are made clear. Jordan is certain that God's values have not changed. Rather, the national community has changed to its detriment. Those who hear Jordan identify "murder" as a destabilizing element in the nation know that she is depicting a rhetorical iceberg. The real damage is being done below the surface by nihilism and the loss of a moral compass. Jordan identifies these trends as "villains" worthy of elimination.

Because she believes that committed individuals and faith communities can resolve America's social ills, her call for responsibility is made to both. In Jordan's considered opinion, the church becomes an interlocutor in its public discourse, raising the difficult and unpopular moral questions. Inevitably, the church challenges the status quo and quickens a reflective and self-critical societal stance. Jordan says that the church is called to voice moral truths and guide the human conscience. Moreover, faith communities provide "the glue of values and principles for the members of this democratic society."[46] Accordingly, she outlines the four key roles of the church in public life.

First, the church is the "primary teacher of moral values and ethical standards"[47] within the community of faith and an exemplar through its members to the community-at-large. Second, the church serves as a sustainer of those in need. Third, the church as an independent entity is not susceptible to the vicissitudes of political life. Therefore, it must raise unpopular positions and participate in public debate about those issues.[48] Finally, Jordan says that the church can elucidate moral values and principles that can mediate between individuals and institutions. The role of mediator and contributor to public policy requires both objectivity and independence.[49]

The first two roles cause no concern, for they fall within the traditional purview of the church. It is the "intrusion" into political and social issues that raises public hackles. Jordan contends that this concern is not well placed.

> A relevant, living, viable church will not shrink from this challenge: it will engage in the issues concerning our basic principles, it will speak out for those who do not have a voice, it will be the source of public forums and debates, throughout which it will raise the moral and ethical questions.... [50]

In her discussion of the key roles of the church, Jordan again uses a word that seems incongruent with vocabularies of faith. That word is *objectivity*. Jordan seems to be translating sectarian concepts into rhetoric with broader meaning and social value. If the church is to be the voice of public theology, Jordan says, it must espouse credible and objective moral claims:

> The church can serve as a mediator on difficult questions of public policy, but to do so it must maintain a reputation for objectivity and independent moral concerns — not partisan propagandists for the left or the right.... Is there a right to health care in America? What is society's responsibility to the poor? Should government be the institution solely responsible for educating our children? What is the right/moral thing to do. [51]

According to Jordan, the civic role of the church cannot be divorced from issues of faith, and issues of faith cannot be divorced from objectivity. She identifies the church, not only as a religious community, but also as the representative voice of God to the faithful, and the faithful to the wider community. The church must be simultaneously a champion of the intangible tenets of faith and an objective advocate of the common good.

Toward a Constructive Public Theology

Jordan suggests that we rethink the meaning of politics as a first step toward a constructive public theology:

> If we view politics in the sinister sense as relating to and describing the crafty and the scheming and the abuse of power

to the detriment of the people, then perhaps the only challenge the Christian would face would be in the outlawing and subsequent abolition of politics.... Until the Christian is able to define politics at a point of relevance to his [her] Christian concern, the debate will not cease, and Christian and political concerns will continue to be mutually exclusive.[52]

The task is to determine the relevance of politics and public life to faith. Commensurate languages facilitate such considerations. When faith perspectives are reconfigured into public discourse, the resulting public theology becomes more than the interpretation of scriptural or doctrinal tenets. This conversion of sacred speech into idiomatic vocabularies neither presages the desire for the wholesale universalization of religious doctrine, nor assumes a universal platform for the dissemination of nonnegotiable faith attestations.

Such a definition would blur the distinction between public theology and evangelism. Rather, public theology acknowledges its rootedness in a particular tradition, but then speaks from and to that tradition and others by translating incommensurate rhetoric into shared language. As Hans-Georg Gadamer indicates, the understanding sought evolves out of a fusion of horizons and meaning structures. Through the mediation of language, interpretation, and dialogue irreconcilable differences can be reassessed and approached from innovative angles.[53] A constructive public theology facilitates a wholeness of mind, body, and spirit, such that the brokenness of the commonweal does not become a permanent chasm.

This is how Jordan defines wholeness: "as the health and wellbeing necessary to fulfill life's potential, and I think of it as having three parts — the physical or body, the mental or mind, and the spiritual or spirit. These are manifested in our lives as good health, long life, religious moral values, education and wisdom."[54] Jordan is not content with a discussion of wholeness in the abstract sense. She philosophically discusses the values and attributes of a fulfilled life, but then connects those ideas to practical needs and political turf. She says: "We need a livable wage, educational opportunity, access to adequate health care, religious and other personal freedom, and the protection afforded by a fair and equitable system of justice. The absence of any one or more of these elements creates barriers to our total health and well-being — wholeness."[55]

The modifiers are the most important concepts in this passage. Jordan has adjusted the American dream to more reasonable proportions to allow for the potential flourishing of a broader base of participants. When capitalism ascended the economic throne, the mantra became: "get as much as you can as fast as you can," "horde, invest, retire early," "you can't be too rich or too thin," or, in the current vernacular, "live large." Jordan suggests a moderation/balance that is almost radical when compared with the prevailing theories of well-being. A livable wage falls far short of the desire for unlimited wealth. Access to health care and educational opportunity does not translate into entitlement legislation.

Jordan admits that her interest in moderation/balance is drawn from Aristotelian theories of the "golden mean." She believes that a balance of competing interests will benefit everyone. Moreover, Jordan assumes that scales tipped in favor of self-interest return to a more balanced tilt when religion assumes a public role as advocate, political provocateur, prophet, and mediator.

She is committed to the idea of balance as a function of religion in public discourse and the formation of public policy. In this respect she says, "The church has a vital and sustaining role in a democratic society. It is my premise that the values embodied in the Judeo-Christian ethic go hand-in-glove with seeking the proper balance."[56] I'm not sure that she's right. Balance is neither the goal nor the doctrinal basis for Christianity. Moreover, if, as liberation theologians have contended for several decades, God is on the side of the poor, then moderation is an unacceptable solution to societal problems.

I am reminded of the consequences that African trickster Esu-Elegba suffers in an effort to mediate (to simultaneously keep each foot) on earthly and divine realms. He inevitably walks with a limp. Theories that seek balance at all cost also inevitably limp. One must decide after analyzing Jordan's speeches whether her public theology pronouncements suffer from this malady.

Jordan's attempts to offer a synthesis of public policy advocacy and uncompromised "kingdom principles" are further complicated by her use of the term access. This is language with more affinity to her faith community. Christianity assumes access to God through Christ, access of the excluded and sinful through redemption, and access to transcendent living through grace. Jordan wants to maintain a balance of competing interests to ensure access to communal well-being.

Her ideas are prospective and aimed at a win/win approach to public life. For Jordan, the first step toward that goal of mutuality is balance. In her view, life is neither a contest of gladiators bent on subduing the weak and infirm nor a sprint for personal gain. If Jordan has her way, neither the church, nor the synagogue, nor the mosque will be excluded from the political realm. While it is yet day, Jordan hopes that the mediating languages of religion, morality, and law will quicken the spirits of the people and encourage reconciling social projects.

And what of the night — the question that Heschel poses at the beginning of this chapter? It is neither a sudden curtain that separates realms of thought or being nor a symbol of dearth or absence. It is an intersection of alternating parts of a whole, a site where voices from public and private realms can welcome otherness.

Chapter 6

Law:
Against the Prevailing Wind

Each generation leaves a legacy to succeeding generations....
[T]hat legacy may be solid, etched as if in stone, or it may
be as fragile as a house of cards, tumbling in the first gust
of wind. — Barbara Jordan[1]

We cannot play ostrich. Democracy cannot flourish amid
fear. Liberty cannot bloom amid hate. Justice cannot take
root amid rage.... We must go against the prevailing wind.
We must dissent from indifference. We must dissent from...
apathy. We must dissent from the fear, the hatred, and the
mistrust. We must dissent from a government that has left its
young without education or hope. We must dissent from the
poverty of vision and the absence of moral leadership. We
must dissent because America can do better, because America
has no choice but to do better. — Thurgood Marshall[2]

The prevailing winds that Jordan and Marshall identify encourage those caught in its gusts to head in a predetermined direction.
Neither Marshall nor Jordan was so inclined. Both believed that
America was not the best that it could be. Both shared a propensity
for straight talk and a belief that the rule of law would prevail over
episodic periods of public turmoil. Even though their assumptions,
rhetorical priorities, and conclusions as to the state of North American jurisprudence differed significantly, both cast their discourse
against the prevailing wind.

The previous chapters devoted to Jordan's ethics identified the
elements of moral discernment, norms gleaned from virtues, and a
concept of moral fulfillment that relies upon shared understand-

ings about the common good. The chapter on public religion explored her translation of faith statements into shared language and repositioned religion as a viable contributor to communal well-being. This sixth chapter focuses on Jordan's reliance on constitutional principles, the contextual and pragmatic aspects of her view of justice, and the translation of both into a thriving national community.

Here I analyze the third interpretive category in Jordan's speeches — law — and compare her theories with the discourse of the late Supreme Court Justice Thurgood Marshall and legal scholars Mari Matsuda and Patricia Williams. Neither Marshall nor Jordan are naïve devotees of the Constitution. Although Marshall spent most of his adult life construing constitutional issues, he never failed to remind all who would listen that nothing could be taken for granted when the supremacy of one race over another has been institutionalized in law. The harsh reality is that if the tree (the system of laws) is poisonous, it will bear poison fruit (laws that render the practices of racial supremacy normative).[3]

Marshall's premise challenges Jordan's passionate commitment to centrist legal ideals. Matsuda's argument for multiple consciousness as a method of legal analysis, and justice as an end rather than a process or procedure, sheds light on Jordan's varying rhetorical vantage points. Patricia Williams refers to the double-voiced responses of marginalized persons to the rigidities of legal proceedings in North America. Each conversation partner contributes a fresh perspective that accents Jordan's approach to issues of justice and law.

Legal Pragmatism

Jurisprudence, the philosophy of law, emerged in the nineteenth century as a discipline that attempts to ascertain the underlying principles of legal rules.[4] In the context of Jordan's speeches, jurisprudence is also a theory of the historical relationship between life and law as a practical activity and transcendent goal.[5] It is this tentative balance of practicality and social optimism that identifies Jordan as a legal pragmatist. She is one who takes experience and consensus building seriously, and believes that justice ought to have practical consequences in the lives of ordinary people.[6]

Legal pragmatism merges traditional, analytical, social policy, and creative approaches to the law. Justice Oliver Wendell Holmes explains the nuances of pragmatism in his book *The Common Law*:

> The life of the law has not been logic: it has been experience. The felt necessities of the time, the prevalent moral and political theories, intuitions of public policy, avowed or unconscious, even the prejudices which judges share.... The law embodies the story of a nation's development through many centuries, and it cannot be dealt with as if it contained only the axioms and corollaries of a book of mathematics.[7]

Pragmatism in a legal context assumes that the law is part of the lifeblood of the nation, a language and experience of engagement with the culture and its institutions. Moreover, pragmatism is often the preferred discourse of "subordinated people" because it is their "indigenous method."[8] Cultural critic and philosopher Cornel West, in his discussion of the resurgence of pragmatism, warns:

> The tradition of pragmatism is in need of a mode of cultural criticism that keeps track of social misery, solicits and channels moral outrage to alleviate it, and projects a future in which the potentialities of ordinary people flourish and flower. The first wave of pragmatism floundered on the rocks of cultural criticism and corporate liberalism. Its defeat was tragic. Let us not permit the second wave of pragmatism to end as a farce.[9]

West commends a prophetic pragmatism based on the concept of critical temper. He defines critical temper as "a way of struggle and democratic faith." For West it is a way of life.[10] In his discourse, legal pragmatism has the potential to alter the course of human events, because it tends to prioritize life, consequences, and human need over formalistic results.

For Jordan, morality and religion suggest particular dispositions that may indeed lead to an improved human landscape. Both morality and religion exhort humankind to avoid the conflicts and pitfalls that beset social interactions. However, neither domain can ensure the protection of social boundaries without the authority of law. Concomitantly, Jordan would argue that law in isolation from religion and morality rarely offers solutions to the iniquity and despair intrinsic to the human condition.[11] Retribution and punishment, rules and enforcement cannot fully redress the wounds that social aberrance inflicts upon the community.[12] In her speeches, the interlocking web of law, ethics, and public religion furnishes a sustainable framework for public discourse and informed responses to social problems. It is also the foundation for her principled approach to law and justice as rhetorical categories and philosophical precursors of the precepts inculcated in the Constitution.

Constitutional Faith

Throughout her public career, Jordan focuses upon constitutional principles that she considers normative and exemplary. She assumes that the authority of the document emanates from a dynamic relationship between text and interpretation, legal rules and the norms that evolve from those rules. Whereas governments promulgate laws, constitutions create and regulate governments. The primacy of constitutional authority is evident when it is considered that laws that contravene constitutional mandates are deemed to be of no effect.

Jordan's feelings about the Constitution are as personal and passionate as her biblical faith. At her funeral, law professor Philip Bobbitt shared the following anecdote: "Many of us learned for the first time in the press accounts following Barbara Jordan's death that she carried with her a small pocket copy of the U.S. Constitution. From some apparently early point...this small pamphlet was always with her."[13] Clearly, Jordan was convinced that the document's reach and potential far exceeded its drafters' intent. Of the Constitution she says, "[t]wo hundred years later, I am not sure that it is not the best. The Constitution is alive and well in America. It is not a lifeless piece of paper resting in a dusty archive. It is a living document and what brings it to life is you, the citizens of this country, who will live out its meaning."[14]

For Jordan, the Constitution is a document that protects religious and individual freedoms while postulating the already/not yet mutuality of a flourishing national community. It is a document that encompasses the idea of a just political order manifested in a written design amenable to the processes of creative interpretation and amendment. Jordan calls the Constitution "the best" but asks for the help of fellow citizens to interpret its meaning. Some of the citizens addressed wondered whether her passion and love for this document had any moral relevance for her own community.

The fact that the law had become an ally of African Americans during the Civil Rights movement did not change the distance between the document and the ordinary lives of the people. Although the Constitution embodies the jurisprudential inclinations of a young nation, more often than not, those inclinations were indistinguishable from (or held hostage by) the interests of a racist, misogynist, and imperialist culture. To be certain, Jordan's trust and reliance on constitutionalism are considered misplaced by those who remember the days of Jim Crow, the Tuskegee syphilis experiments, and judicial construals that sanctioned and at times encouraged abuse.[15]

As the gap between rhetorical promises and actual practices grew wider in marginalized communities, the Bible (and other culturally relevant spiritual referents) supplanted the Constitution as a model of justice and source of authority. Biblical/spiritual expositions of freedom, moral guidelines, and assurance of a better future offered everything that the Constitution had denied minorities.[16] Jordan is aware of this gap between performance and reality, yet persists in her heartfelt reclamation of constitutional principles.

To radically love the Constitution, a document that excluded minorities from its inception, is an act that potentially transforms the lover and the loved as well as observers of the phenomenon. It is no wonder that Jordan's startling appropriation of the founding document during the Watergate hearings ignited interest. This is how Jordan expresses her faith. She says: "My faith in the Constitution is whole, it is complete, it is total. I am not going to sit here and be an idle spectator to the subversion, the destruction of the Constitution."[17]

The issue is not whether her "faith" is warranted; rather, it is whether this faith is necessary to her analysis. Legal scholar Harold Berman says that it is. He encourages performative acts that personalize the substance and spirit of the law: "It is no overstatement, therefore, to speak of fidelity or faithfulness to law. This is essentially the same kind of dramatic response to the sacred, to the ultimate purpose of life, that is characteristic of religious faith. Law, like religion, originates in celebration and loses its vitality when it ceases to celebrate."[18] Berman's use of the term "celebrate" assumes that the dramatic and ritual acts integral to law and religion continue to revitalize both realms.

Jordan "celebrates" the Constitution in her speeches. She contends that it is a document that describes, in ideal terms, a level playing field for political endeavor and a safe harbor for religious expression and public discourse. Accordingly, her rhetoric in support of the Constitution should not be misconstrued as mindless patriotism. Jordan has "faith" in the ability of the people to transcend the limitations of the framers' intent through moral imagination and action. She also has faith in the ability of the people to claim the right to construct a more perfect pluralistic union. In that respect she says: "We are proud that we, each and every one of us, are the 'We the People' who ordained and established the Constitution of the United States of America. That is, we created the government and it exists to serve us. That is our faith."[19]

This quotation helps to clarify Jordan's statements about "constitutional faith." Evidently, the faith that she has in the Constitution is prospective. The faith that she refers to is "the substance of things hoped for, the evidence of things not seen" articulated in Holy Scripture.[20] Jordan uses the language of faith in a way that emphasizes its imminence, power, and constructive potential. Such power is available to everyone as a latent but feasible option.

Just as Jordan recognizes the benefit of translating religious language into public discourse, she also wants to broaden the meaning of patriotism so that disparate and even conflictual opinions can also claim a faith in national ideals. Moreover, she encourages active interpretation as a crucial component of constitutional faith. For the Constitution is not a self-interpreting document.[21] If one can consider that interpretation is the art of construing, then "there are as many plausible readings of the constitutional document as there are versions of *Hamlet*."[22]

Those who resist Jordan's interpretation-activism by insisting on deference to the "framers' intent" assume a simplicity of legal purpose that belies history. The Constitution is a contested document, the outcome of a process of negotiation and bargaining. As such, it becomes more difficult to attribute a singular intention to the framers. Moreover, certain key words had different meanings in the eighteenth century. For example, the term "equality" in that era did not conflict with the institution of slavery.[23] This interpretive incongruity raises the issue of legal perspective and the viability of multiple consciousness as a jurisprudential method.[24] Patricia Williams refers to this altered vantage point as "multiple voice, double-voicedness — the shifting consciousness which is the daily experience of people of color and of women."[25]

As discussed by Professor Matsuda, multiple consciousness allows perspectival and interpretive flexibility. This is the same flexibility that allowed the framers to use the term "equality" in a way that excluded gender, race, and ethnicity. However, Matsuda is clear that flexibility does not imply "the random ability to see the world from all points of view."[26] Rather, Matsuda defines multiple consciousness as a "new jurisprudence," a deliberate choice to see the world from the standpoint of the oppressed.[27]

Although the formal application of multiple consciousness to law may be new, its historical and practical use by persons of color is not. W. E. B. Du Bois first identified the liminal state of "double consciousness" in *The Souls of Black Folks*.[28] He describes a state of being that is not a choice. Rather, it is a safety valve and survival technique for those locked into positions of inferiority because of racial designations. Matsuda acknowledges Du Bois's specific and contextual use and then expands its potential application by recognizing multiple consciousness in the Grimké sisters. The sisters choose to stand with the oppressed.[29] In both instances, solutions to intractable problems become accessible when perspectives are varied and creative.

To be certain, human relations tend to be complex even in the simplest of times. We live on varied levels, victimized by some traits and privileged by others. To clarify this concept, I find it necessary to make broad references to generalized human categories. For instance, some white women struggle with issues of gender bias but have access to race privilege. Some black men are shackled by race but exercise gender privilege in their homes and in the churches. Some black women seem to have no privilege card to play until they enter a global context where their class and economic well-being become the privilege that separates them from the Two-Thirds World. When you add issues of sexual orientation to this collapsible grid of power and privilege, the hierarchies shift yet again.

Jordan would agree with Matsuda that categories of privilege and victimization are not static but are negotiated within the construct of race, class, gender/sexuality. Multiple consciousness takes seriously these multiple realities. In the legal context, it encourages a hermeneutic of suspicion and a refreshing interpretive volatility. It also helps to explicate Jordan's constitutional allegiance. She is speaking on many levels from varied points of view that exceed the limits of race.

Like Jordan, Matsuda claims the Constitution as her own. Accordingly her voice is important to Jordan's claims. Matsuda says:

> I am choosing as my heritage the 200 years of struggle by poor and working people, by Native Americans, by people of color, for dignified lives in this nation. I can claim as my own the Constitution that my father swore to uphold and defend.... It was not written for me, but I can make it my own, using my chosen consciousness as a woman and a person of color to give substance to those tantalizing words "equality" and "liberty."[30]

Thus it can be said that Matsuda's and Jordan's "constitutional faith" amounts to more than a thin sheen of hope layered upon the bare bones of abstract jurisprudential theory. When considered in synthesis with their own moral and religious sensibilities, faith in the Constitution is personal. This creative dynamism can potentially overcome the facade of legal neutrality and contributes to enlightened constitutional interpretations.

Supreme Court Justice Thurgood Marshall also shared Jordan's belief that the Constitution required the continued reconstructive efforts of an informed and diverse populace.[31] In an article written for the *Houston Lawyer* entitled "Reflections on the Constitution," Jordan quotes Marshall's remarks:

> I do not believe that the meaning of the Constitution was "fixed" at the Philadelphia Convention. Nor do I find the wisdom, foresight, and sense of justice exhibited by the framers particularly profound. To the contrary, the government they devised was defective from the start, requiring several amendments, a civil war, and momentous social transformations to attain the system of constitutional government, and its respect for the individual freedoms and human rights, we hold as fundamental today. When contemporary Americans cite "the Constitution," they invoke a concept that is vastly different from what the framers barely began to construct two centuries ago.[32]

Marshall and Jordan approach the Constitution in very different ways. He hopes to divest the Constitution of its mythical trappings in order to set it in a more realistic context. Jordan views the document as a point of convergence for the critical synergy of religious, moral, and political ideals. She is convinced that a multicultural community can make justice relevant to their needs if they get involved with matters of public policy. Moreover, she believes that the Constitution is worthy of their personal commitment and faith. Jordan's famous statement about faith in the Constitution evokes a sense of the sacred.

By contrast, Marshall refers to faith as that necessary help in times of trouble. At a dinner in his honor, he talks about the "faith" of minorities in a system that rarely works for their benefit. He says, "Why do I say, with faith we can make it? What the hell else have we had but faith."[33] Jordan was a firm believer in the myth of liberal progress; Marshall wasn't always so certain about its value. On one occasion he said, "People say we are better off today. Better than what?"[34]

Both Marshall and Jordan were firsthand observers of the shifting political and legal winds. Both witnessed deeply entrenched racial bias supported by the rule of law "morph" into the insidious and ostensibly neutral policies that accomplished similar purposes. Although both have faith in the law, Marshall's faith is tempered with a healthy dose of skepticism. Marshall as advocate and adjudicator recognizes and resists the inequities. Jordan as congressional legislator and politician is more familiar with the processes of debate and compromise. Jordan and Marshall make different rhetorical choices, but both are working within the system to effect change.

Just as Jordan's religious faith challenges assumptions about the roles of Christians and the church in the body politic, her constitutional faith critiques and reflexively engages assumptions about the national community. Her goals require her to respond to voices past and present that still influence the nation's agenda. In Jordan's speeches, the Constitution has a rhetorical value and voice. To understand this phenomenon, consider James Boyd White's characterization of "voice" in another preeminent national document, the Declaration of Independence:

> It is not a person's voice, not even that of a committee, but the unanimous voice of thirteen united states and their people. It addresses a universal audience, nothing less than humankind itself — located neither in space nor in time. The voice is universal too, for it purports to know about the course of human events and to be able to discern what becomes necessary as a result of changing circumstances.[35]

If the voice of the Constitution is heard by Jordan, it is heard in a language of lofty ideals that are occasionally co-opted by the interests of the dominant culture. However, such interests exercise control only for as long as contradictory voices remain silent. In a speech entitled "Recapturing the Spirit of America," Jordan identifies the voices of faith in the following poetic excerpt:

> The voices of faith and hope should rise in a great crescendo and remind these prophets (of doom)...of what America is all about....It is part of the spirit of this country to recognize ...all human potential....America needs advocates who can

restore faith in its dream and promise; who can help affirm and actualize its historical commitments to its citizenry.[36]

Once again Jordan uses the word "faith" to convey the political and moral ideals of the nation. Considered in this light, Jordan's faith in the Constitution assumes the reconstructive contributions of a diverse citizenry. In this regard, Professor Bobbitt agrees; he says, "Without the resort to individual conscience, law itself is arid and will not long be able to call on our devotion."[37]

On more than one occasion, Jordan acts as the "constitutional conscience" of the nation. She is convinced that the government represents the institutionalized will of the people it serves.[38] Moreover, the Constitution embodies a promise of justice. The framers described a union of precisely conceived allocations of power but neglected the issues of pluralism that existed from the document's inception. Now, Jordan raises the possibility of a new community made up of diverse cultures linked nationally and globally by concepts of justice as fairness, caring, and commitment.

Justice as Daily Practice

Jordan was a practicing lawyer before she became a legislator and educator. As a consequence, her speeches on justice focus on the pragmatic concerns of the people. In a speech entitled "Justice" she says: "Justice is one of the first words in our Constitution, one of the first principles upon which this nation was founded. It is something that we have been working very hard to achieve for the last two centuries, yet, today, we are uncertain about what it is and how to achieve it."[39]

Jordan is addressing the National Attorneys General Convention:

> [Despite] enormous amounts of human and monetary capital in building our system of justice...we are unsure whether it can achieve the desired results....As a result, every aspect of our system of justice is being questioned from how it is organized, to the techniques we use to prevent crime, to the very philosophy upon which it is based.[40]

Although Jordan's remarks about justice refer specifically to criminal law, she uses this occasion to raise a difficult issue, namely, "the inability of our system of justice to preserve the social fabric which binds this nation together."[41] This is not a problem specific to Western liberal democracies. Historically, Greek and Hebrew concepts of justice also struggled to create a balance between the objectives of revenge and reconciliation. Jordan realizes that the North American system of laws has not escaped from the horns of that dilemma.

She is also aware that the issue of justice in America cannot be relegated to the courts or the legislators. Her intent is to initiate public dialogue about an issue that will be an important subject of discussion throughout her life. One month before her death, she reconsiders the issue in a speech entitled "The Obligations of Inter-Generational Justice." This speech shows evidence that her thinking has been refined considerably since her pronouncements about justice in 1976. In the earlier speech, Jordan concerns herself with the nuts and bolts of a functioning justice system. In this later speech, justice is clearly identified as a virtue synonymous with fairness.

According to Jordan, our system seeks to guarantee that "each citizen gets justice and justice is denied no one. What is justice? Justice is fairness. It is the first virtue of all human institutions."[42] However, for Jordan, fairness does not subsume the entire meaning of "justice." Jordan also associates the concept with caring, social responsibility, and joint action. Of course, John Rawls inscribed the phrase "justice as fairness" on the culture in 1971 in his book *A Theory of Justice*.[43] However, rather than transpose Rawls's ideas intact, Jordan extracts the flavor of his language without delving into the specifics of his hypothetical concept of procedural justice. It is the word fairness that Jordan is concerned with and not the content of Rawls's theory. Her theory of justice is a medley of phrases and concepts gleaned from jurists, scholars, family, and friends, filtered through her own unique creative processes.

At this point it would be prudent to explain how Jordan defines justice. However, there are two primary reasons that one cannot assert maxims or systematic elements to frame her discourse on this subject. First, incompletion is a recurring motif in Jordan's speeches. She is not one to settle on definitions. When Jordan convenes a conversation about justice, she invites her listeners/ readers to enter a rich but transitory colloquy. Second, Jordan was only fifty-nine when she died. The dialogue about justice in a multiethnic context was still relatively new. Her speeches are the disparate but carefully crafted repositories of her thought.[44]

Notwithstanding those caveats, an analysis of the speeches reveals that Jordan considers justice to be the outward manifestation of inner values. These are values that can be practically applied in everyday life and in the courts. For Jordan, justice as fairness and as a practical value cannot stand alone; it requires the spiritual corrective of justice as caring. In this regard, she says: "The philosophical debate between people and numbers for the United States of American had always contained a component for caring for the more vulnerable among our citizenry. We have cared because we felt an obligation to care."[45]

Jordan touts caring not as a sentiment, but as an element of justice and law. She argues that it is a duty, a virtue, and a choice. She says that our only real choice is to allow the nation to proceed toward economic well-being while continuing to care for the less fortunate. This is Jordan at her best. She sets high standards and expects everyone within hearing of her voice to get involved. For Jordan, the entire issue is a matter of will. The responsibility for a functioning and compassionate society rests with us, not the government, but the collective will of moral individuals.[46]

Jordan envisions an orderly community of persons who cannot escape human, civic, and religious attachments. In a speech that invokes memories of ancient Israel's demand for a king and Samuel's antimonarchical advice, she depicts the historical desire for laws that will benefit public interests:[47]

> Maybe it began with George Washington and his little known aristocratic desire to be an American king. Or maybe it began before that with Thomas Jefferson writing into the law of our land that every citizen had not only the right but the privilege to pursue happiness. . . . [S]omewhere in our weaning we began or rather never lost our desire for strong national lead-

ership — for strong centralized authority — for a father figure
at the helm of state who could guarantee happiness.⁴⁸

Jordan argues that happiness is not some ethereal state of being that descends upon seekers. It is a consequence of civic and
personal participation and effort. Because happiness cannot prevail amid social or personal chaos, systems of justice provide the
stability necessary for optimal human relations. Jordan believes
that a just society is a practical cooperative alliance of free and
equal persons who can be either beneficiaries or victims of the system of laws, depending on their levels of participation in the civic
project.

Ultimately, Jordan expresses her belief that the North American
system of justice reflects the best and worst of human endeavors.
However, even though society is in disarray, sociopolitical fissures
are deep, and commitments to public life have eroded, Jordan is
optimistic. She posits the possibility of a flourishing national community that synthetically embodies the disparate and conflictual
elements of society. Jordan's proposed community is bound by
shared values, a site of kinetic transformations, and constantly
shifting boundaries.

This is the task that Jordan assigns to law — to act as a mediating force between the elements of good and evil. Her just
community requires the complementary action of human agency
and the transcendent intervention of God's grace through the
Holy Spirit still active in the world. Finally, Jordan realizes that
the justice system, laws, and institutions contribute to the moral
"fingerprint" of her generation. Because these institutions serve
as historical artifacts of the moral propensities of a given society, Jordan urges us to push the limits of social theory to create
possibilities of transcendence where none exist.

I began this chapter with Jordan's and Marshall's references to
the prevailing wind, a force to be reckoned with by all who in-
tend to impress their inclinations toward justice. The phrase is
not limited to resistance but includes a cognizance of relationality
expressed by orators like Native American spiritualist Black Elk:

> Hear me four quarters of the world, a relative I am. Give me
> the strength to walk the soft earth, a relative to all that is.

Give me the eyes to see and the strength to understand that I
may be like you. With your power only can I face the winds.[49]

This excerpt emphasizes spiritual empowerment as an important factor in human endeavors. Both Marshall and Jordan agree
that despite the shortcomings of North American systems of justice, there is hope. This hope is expressed in the call for America
to "do better." The next chapter examines how "doing better"
would look in the configuration of a multiethnic community. Here,
Jordan's speeches on community are considered in dialogue with
Martin Luther King Jr.'s beloved community and Victor Turner's
conception of *communitas*. As in the preceding chapters, the
speeches emphasize connectedness, accountability, and the moral
flourishing of the national community. Jordan's theories of law and
justice resist the rigid contours of static institutions, invoking instead the creative and malleable tendencies of an idea attendant to
the wishes of the people. This is a view of justice that leans against
the prevailing wind.

Part Four

The Vision

Chapter 7

A Beloved, National, and Transcendent Community: Still Not Unthinkable

I say all of this . . . so that you know that what I have written, and what I write from now on, is not based on the assumption of idyllic possibilities or innocent assessments of the true nature of life. But rather, my own personal view that . . . it is still not unthinkable to me that the human race might just do what apes never will: impose the reason for life on life.

— LORRAINE HANSBERRY[1]

Victor Turner contends that "every memorable play or novel is about apparently irresolvable moral contradictions."[2] Therefore, it is fitting that this final chapter begins with a quotation from Lorraine Hansberry's play *To Be Young Gifted and Black*. In her own words, this play is a celebration of playwright Hansberry's life. As the producer notes in the script, it is "a celebration of one writer's view of the human spirit."[3] As such, it is also a celebration of contradictions, impossibilities, and indefatigable human aspirations.

Likewise, Jordan's speeches encapsulate her view of the communal disposition of the human spirit. Through the overlapping themes of ethics, public religion, and law, she demonstrates her belief in a symbiotic social order.[4] Ultimately, this perspective culminates in Jordan's notion of the national community. For Jordan, an ideal national community is the model of moral fulfillment. In this chapter, I consider the meaning of "community" in Jordan's speeches and in current discourse, and juxtapose her model of community to Martin Luther King Jr.'s beloved community and to the transcendent elements of Victor Turner's *communitas*. King's and Turner's concepts are considered symbolic modalities that facilitate an understanding of Jordan's unfinished vision. In the end, Jordan's model of community emerges as a rhetorical summation of her religious, moral, and legal imperatives.

I also consider whether the very idea of community is an outdated goal in the current political climate. Radical individualists argue that community discourse is subversive to their interests.[5] They consider individual rights to be the linchpin of a flourishing society and fear that their interests will be lost in a black hole of communitarian parity.[6] To others, communal or communitarian language reflects the actual state of human existence. The perfection of that state of being is considered an ultimate goal of human striving.

Elizabeth Bounds identifies the attraction/repulsion syndrome that pervades discussions of community. She argues that "the unprecedented depth and breadth of current capitalism have created conditions of fragmentation and alienation where it is difficult to develop stable relational identities."[7] Her solution to this dilemma is a richly layered model of society marked by its pluralism and civic participation.[8] Bounds believes that this multifarious concept of community has the potential to assuage the trepidation that the rhetoric of homogeneity engenders. This will not be an easy feat, because liberal and communitarian discourse is polarized around the issues of character, moral education, and the unencumbered self.[9]

If cultural mutuality is to be achieved at any level, it may ultimately be more productive to bridge these epistemological camps in the language of the public good and public concerns. Sociologist Daniel Bell advocates this approach. For Bell, the problem is how to sustain a commonweal that mediates between the extreme options of an imposed governmentally determined good and the chaos of culture wars waged at every level of society.[10] Bell makes the point that public policy must be distinguished from the common good, and that policy cannot be antithetical to the needs or free expressions of the individual.[11]

Bell seeks a delicate balance between personal autonomy and

common goals. He also alludes to a state of being akin to moral flourishing that characterizes this objective. What is this elusive state of mutual well-being that permeates Jordan's rhetoric and Martin Luther King Jr.'s dreams, but defies quantification? Bell argues that it is the attempt to grasp "a philosophy in something of the old sense, a love of or yearning after a good, rather than a received or imposed good."[12] When public philosophy satisfies this human need, it draws adherents through persuasion rather than authoritarianism. Essentially, Bell argues for an approach that Jordan consistently uses: "the attracting of agreements rather than the suggestion of imposed solutions."[13] The elements that create this attraction are as illusive as the reasons why one theatrical production fails while another succeeds.

An equally thorny problem that arises during colloquies on the issue of community is the veiled desire for conformity that shadows the ostensible moral idealism. After all is said and done, there is the sense that what is really sought is sameness and the obliteration of difference. On this point, Jordan's rhetoric is conflicted. On the one hand, her view of community does not assume the elimination of differences. She says, "It is not easy to keep pace with America. Her people are diverse and any thought of homogeneity as a goal is useless and futile."[14] On the other hand, she ascribes to an implicit conformity to certain symbols of civic order such as "English" as the official language of the nation.[15] These disparities in Jordan's rhetoric may reflect the difficulties inherent in the dialectical tension between individual rights and common goals. It may also be the result of the unfinished state of her theory.

Ultimately, Jordan's speeches disclose her realization that communities develop out of the complex components of human striving and the unique experiences that individuals bring to that effort. In this respect, her own experiences of community influence her approach to the national community. Growing up in a segregated but vital and sustaining neighborhood allows Jordan to meld race, place, and geography into a rich resource for her future theories. She considers community to be a component of society that combines the elements of locus and transcendence.

By contrast, cultural analyst Maffesoli distinguishes "society" from "community" according to the discernible reasons for each

social unit to exist. Maffesoli believes that societies are concerned
with the historical continuum, whereas communities exhaust themselves in the act of self-creation.[16] Although I am not certain that
the differences are so clearly defined, some of the elements of
community that he identifies are basic and familiar. According to
Maffesoli, "The communal ethic has the simplest of foundations:
warmth, companionship — physical contact with one another...
it is by force of circumstance: because of circumstance; because
of proximity... because there is a sharing of the same territory
(real or symbolic) that the communal idea and its ethical corollary
are born."[17]

This theory of community emphasizes the "crystallization of
feeling in the act of being together."[18] Other descriptions focus less
upon physical connections, shared sentiments, and territory, prefer-
ring instead to posit the idea of community as an ideal collective of
diametric concepts.[19] Still others focus on the religious function of
a community:

> Communities, especially historically extended communities
> ... are the principal matrices and repositories of religious an-
> swers to such questions: Who are we? Where did we come
> from? What is our origin, our beginning? Where are we go-
> ing? What is our destiny, our end? What is the meaning of
> suffering? of evil? of death? And there is the cardinal ques-
> tion, the question that comprises many of the others: Is the
> world ultimately meaningful or, instead, ultimately bereft of
> meaning, meaningless, absurd?[20]

I do not agree that these questions are necessarily religious. To the
contrary, they are the questions that pervade all facets of human
life. Jordan addresses these concerns by structuring her speeches
in such a way that the quest for answers can be viewed as a purposeful end and not a means to an end. This framework allows
her to tap into the energy and resolve of a yearning people and to
translate that yearning into praxis.

Jordan has learned from the mistakes of the Great Society — too
much idealism, too little pragmatism. By the time of her death, she
is advocating the implementation of reachable goals while maintaining the lodestar of transcendent ideals. However, this attention

to the details of a viable national community is not typical of Jordan's earlier speeches. Her first speeches on community initiatives tend to eschew details in favor of broad philosophical propositions. Moreover, it is clear that the model that she proposes is neither a finished blueprint nor a perfect prototype. It is an ideal that she offers for public contestation and consideration. As early as 1977, she says:

> Is a national community probable? A negative response to that question appears to border on certainty. A little more than a year ago, I issued a call for the development of a sense of national community. The call warned of the dangers of divisiveness and sectionalism. The words I spoke evoked thunderous applause. Today, a year and two months later the follow-up question is: "What were those people applauding"?[21]

The answer to Jordan's question is that they were probably applauding her tough-minded approach to the diverging interests of what Philip Bobbitt calls "a society that is becoming increasingly characterized by a pervasive goal-sapping cynicism."[22] King faces a similar challenge; the community may be spiritually beloved, but it must also sustain the economic and political needs of the people.

The Beloved Community

> For [King], the beloved community was the goal of the civil rights movement and of the human struggle as a whole.[23]

> King held that humans are not individuals who are completely self-sufficient but social beings who find authentic existence through social contact and social relations under the guidance of a personal God who works for universal wholeness.[24]

King's beloved community is an unfinished amalgam of religious, moral, experiential, and philosophical influences. His vision of a transfigured social order assumes that moral rectitude can balance and restore a nation at odds with itself. Moreover, King's ideals

extend beyond national borders to encompass "a world-wide fel-
lowship that lifts neighborly concern beyond one's tribe, race, class
and nation."[25]

Certainly, King led a movement that changed history. However,
it is often difficult to separate the documentary history of a peaceful reformer from the one-dimensional and almost mythic image
of King as the black Gandhi.[26] Of late, scholars have brought
more realistic images of King and his beloved community to public attention. Historian Lewis V. Baldwin gives an account of the
international scope of King's beloved community and its implications for South African reform.[27] Historian Stewart Burns presents
King as a man caught up in events inspired by an egalitarian
core of committed persons from every strata of the black community.[28] King seizes the moment. However, he is often reacting to
events controlled by grassroots activists. As the movement ignites
in Montgomery and becomes a national and then international
vision, King's perspective changes.

There is an edge to his rhetoric by the time he writes *Where
Do We Go from Here?: Chaos or Community*. He is beset by
competing social forces, radicalized black power advocates, and
a widening war in Vietnam. Moreover, he is losing faith in the
possibility that a reconciled community can be constructed on a
foundation of legal victories wrested from a reluctant majority. In
a very real sense, legal victories have mitigated the most obvious
forms of publicly manifested racism, but have left untouched sub-
stantive areas of human relations. King says, "Laws are passed
in a crisis mood after a Birmingham or a Selma, but no sub-
stantial fervor survives the formal signing of legislation."[29] On
another occasion in support of judicial intervention, King says,
"Judicial decrees may not change the heart, but they can restrain
the heartless."[30]

Like Jordan, King contends that law alone cannot ameliorate
social problems or supply the sole framework for his communal
ideal. Although he recognizes a disparity between secular and sacred realms, his public theology relies upon the teachings of Jesus
to undergird the beloved community. Lewis Baldwin describes this
ideological marker of the beloved community as a Christocentric
but not Christomonistic construct.[31] King understands that his

Christian context will be informed by and in conversation with other religions and cultures in the multicultural "world house."[32] The very act of using Christian principles in a secular context requires translation of those precepts into more "public" language. Accordingly, Christ is considered in universal terms as the progenitor of peace, justice, and wholeness for all people.

For King, the mediating factor between incommensurate belief systems is the concept of love. He also considers the beloved community to be dependent on a revolution of values — a radical shift in moral perspectives. These are the changes he envisions for the beloved community: a higher priority for people and their needs, a lesser emphasis on possessions; serious consideration of justice and fairness; and adjustments to the inequities related to wealth and poverty.[33]

Theologian and legal scholar Anthony E. Cook argues that King leaned toward democratic socialism at the end of his life. King is reported to have made the following statement: "Something is wrong with capitalism as it now stands in the United States. We are not interested in being integrated into this value structure. Power must be relocated; a radical redistribution of power must take place."[34] King's vision of the beloved community was evolving more substantively to include a guaranteed minimum income, guaranteed employment, and a redistribution of wealth. This is a view of community that stands in contrast to Jordan's belief in the market economy and is a view of King that is seldom emphasized by the media.

Finally, King says that the beloved community is the only viable alternative to anarchy, for justice denied will seek redress no matter the cost. King says, "All over the globe men are revolting against old systems of exploitation and oppression, and out of the wombs of a frail world, new systems of justice and equality are being born."[35] He also says: "We still have a choice today: nonviolent coexistence or violent co-annihilation. This may well be mankind's last chance to choose between chaos and community."[36] King knows that nothing is as inexorable as birth or death or the quest for justice. The beloved community is justice enacted. The beloved community is an inevitability. There will either be a birth or a disaster.

The National Community

Jordan proposes the idea of a national community in her first keynote speech before the Democratic National Convention:

> We are a people in search of a national community. We believe in equality for all and privileges for none.... We believe that the people are the source of all governmental power... providing each citizen with every opportunity to participate. We believe that the government which represents the authority of all the people, not just one interest group... has an obligation to... remove those obstacles which would block individual achievement.[37]

In this excerpt, Jordan launches a search for community that assumes its existence and its elusiveness. However, it is a search that does not require movement. Jordan offers clues to the immediacy of the idea. On several occasions, particularly during her Watergate speech, Jordan hints that community may be found within the language of the Preamble to the Constitution. What is community, if it is not "We the people"? Unfortunately, Jordan's call for a national community is issued to a skeptical audience. The turbulent sixties and midseventies have produced a national aversion for shared concerns and public discourse. The unspoken understanding is that such efforts inevitably led to chaos. Who can refute the evidence? Even the most visionary leaders have come to no good end. However, Jordan argues that contrary to the prevailing belief, it is not mutuality that threatens to dislodge the "ship of state" but private interests, greed, and tribalism. Jordan says: "Given a choice, people will choose what is in their best interest. That does not presuppose that the choices made will be against the national interest. We are, in fact, one nation and a conglomerate of interdependent people. The interdependence gives us hope for the emergence and ultimate survival of a true national community."[38]

In her first keynote speech before the Democratic Convention, Jordan continues her effort to identify the real enemy of national interests. This 1976 speech inspires but is short on details as to how Jordan's national community will become a reality. However, she accomplishes what she set out to do, which is to raise the possibility of joint action that will not devolve into street fighting, slogan shouting, or protest. Then, in a later speech entitled "Equality, Liberty, and the Pursuit of Community in America," Jordan sets forth a more detailed explanation of the national community and couples the concept of community with equality and liberty. Jordan considers these concepts to be empty vessels ready for the infilling of public ideas.

She also considers it unfortunate that in the Western context, the terms *equality* and *liberty* have become synonymous with autonomy and individualism. Jordan begins by using a conventional definition of community as "a body of people living in one place or district or country and considered as a whole."[39] She goes on to say that this definition is unsatisfactory because the word *community* implies so much more.[40]

Jordan is content not to offer an ad hoc image of the national community; she instead engages the thoughts and theories of other philosophers and analysts. This approach reinforces the idea that she is not settled on the definitions or boundaries of community.

Jordan quotes Jeremy Bentham's definition of community as a starting point. Bentham describes community as a "fictitious body, composed of the individual persons who are considered as constituting...its members."[41] However, Jordan agrees with public philosopher Walter Lippmann, that Bentham's definition is static and therefore too limited to be a definitive depiction of community. For Jordan, a national community is a dynamic and fluid synthesis of disparate elements.

She offers three attributes of community identified by Scott Peck in his book *The Different Drum: Community Making and Peace*, including: inclusivity, commitment, and consensus.[42] Although it seems that this is not one of her more creative speeches, in fact an innovative strategy is evident. When Jordan appropriates ideas, definitions, and theories of community from various sources, she models the process of community building. The process of combining these diverse elements simulates the aggregative process that eventually will constitute the national community. Jordan seems to say that if the national community can be rhetorically constructed, it can be imagined and brought into being.

Ultimately, Jordan contends that it is the pursuit of community that is most promising. She believes that like the pursuit of peace, or happiness, or equality, the pursuit of community changes the character and mindset of the pursuer. When will a pursuit of the national community end? Jordan says this: "We will know when community is realized. Our sense of well-being will be heightened. Our minds, our hearts, ourselves will open. We will laugh and cry and love. That's worth a successful pursuit."[43] In this excerpt, Jordan provides a glimpse of community that surpasses sociopolitical boundaries.

In a speech entitled "Nations in Community," Jordan, like King, broadens the scope of her vision to include international relationships:

> This country and its people can no longer act as if it was a nation state, isolated as a geographic entity — denying global relationships. When the United States policy of isolation and non-involvement was shattered by Pearl Harbor, we knew at once and for all time that unilateral action and separate thinking had come to an end. . . . [W]e survived not only with the realization of a community of nations, but with the awesome responsibility of leader of the free world.[44]

Jordan's view of community is both internal and external. It is linked to moral sensibilities, transcendence, and love. She is not alone when she makes a connection between social processes and religious precepts. King makes a similar claim in his beloved community, and like King, Jordan also envisions kindred communities. However, the primary difference between them lies in their approach to national values.

In his "Riverside" speech, King positions himself as a leader opposed to a static view of American symbols of freedom and justice. When he first entered the public sphere, he engaged the public imagination and garnered respect for his resolute moral positions. Although he was challenging the bastions of white supremacy, his discourse placed him in the mainstream of North American values. Moreover, he was peaceful and articulate. However, his stance on economic empowerment and Vietnam represented a radical expansion of his vision of community. King was on a collision course with the systems of domination. He is reported to have told writer David Halberstam:

> For years I labored with the idea of reforming existing insti-
> tutions of society. A little change here, a little change there.
> Now I feel quite differently. I think you've got to have a re-
> construction of the entire society, a revolution of values and
> perhaps the nationalization of some major industries.[45]

King had a moral consensus for the Civil Rights movement.
However, he had none for his call for economic justice and an
end to the war in Vietnam. At the end of his life, he argued that
racism and colonialism were not the missteps of a just and righ-
teous nation, but in actuality, examples of an evil system working
as it was intended.[46] By contrast, Jordan is committed to every aspect of the civic order. She considers violations of human rights in
North America to be lapses of justice and judgment that can be
overcome through a reinstatement of moral priorities and public
involvement. As for the economic injustice that concerned King,
Jordan says: "We can have constructive capitalism where people
work and earn and where people also are not isolated sick, dying,
destitute, homeless. None of that."[47]

Although Jordan does not discuss her view of constructive capitalism in detail, she seems to seek a balance of capitalism and care.
Moreover, she believes that her goal of community can be achieved
through law, public virtue, secularization, and an allegiance to civic
and constitutional precepts. King's beloved community focuses on
justice, civil disobedience, and Christian precepts translated into a
radically reordered social and economic order. However, both Jordan and King reach toward a religious, moral, and legal mutuality
that transcends cultural boundaries.

The Transcendent Community

In both the beloved and national communities, transcendence is an
important but elusive element, for rhetorical propositions cannot
subsume all that there is to know or say about intentional human
communities. Turner says:

> [It is] my view that any society that hopes to be imperishable
> must carve out for itself a piece of space and a period of time

in which it can look honestly at itself. This honesty is not that of the scientist, who exchanges the honesty of his ego for the objectivity of his gaze. It is rather akin to the supreme honesty of the creative artist who, in his [her] presentations on the stage in the book, on canvas, in marble, in music, or in towers and houses, reserves to him [her] self the privilege of seeing straight what all cultures build crooked.[48]

The public orator shares this capacity to delineate triumphs and foibles of culture and to carve out spaces of honesty. Within the boundaries of rhetoric, the idea of community can be nurtured, modeled, and performed. Turner captures this elusive and creative idea of community in the term *communitas*. He defines *communitas* as "a relationship between concrete, historical, and idiosyncratic individuals."[49] Turner also says that *communitas* is "a generic human bond, a relational quality of full unmediated communication, even communion, between definite and determinate human identities...which arises spontaneously in all kinds of groups, situations, and circumstances."[50] As exciting as this proposition may sound, Turner warns that *communitas* events may eventually be transformed into normative jural-political systems.[51] There is the constant tension between structure and antistructure, order and its potentially anarchic opposite.

A brief explanation of the theory is warranted. In an ethnographic context, *communitas* is an egalitarian state associated with ritual and liminal rites of passage. In a Western context, the theory facilitates a view of society as processive and amenable to creative revision. According to Turner, there are three forms of *communitas:* existential or spontaneous, normative, and ideological. The ideological (or utopian) form of *communitas* comes closest to describing an optimal state of human flourishing. Spontaneous *communitas* is described as approximating a "happening." Normative versions are systematized and organized. It is in the ideological communitas that Turner believes free reign is given to "the cultural realm of myth, ritual, and symbol."[52]

The nexus between Jordan's national community (nations in community) and Turner's *communitas* becomes clear as he articulates his theory of "We the people." Turner borrows this terminology from Martin Buber, who speaks of an "essential we — a powerful concept of relationality."⁵³ This is a view of human relations that is recurrent in each model of community reviewed in this chapter. Both Turner and Jordan see the "essential we" as liminal and dynamic. For Jordan, this phrase is a metaphor for a shared life that is foundational for a flourishing moral community. She believes that a community that transcends the anomalies of difference can be rhetorically envisioned because "we are all a common race. The humanness of us all is the basis for this commonness; this humanness transcends boundaries of language, custom, origin, and geography. These are qualities common to all people."⁵⁴ Common traits in respectful alliance with cultural and personal differences are also intrinsic elements of the beloved, national, and transcendent communities. The ultimate goal is to balance the kinetic dynamism of a spontaneous or ideological community with civic structural dimensions.⁵⁵

The visions of community discussed in this chapter consider the nature of public life and the elements of virtue and justice necessary to facilitate moral flourishing. King struggles to rectify injustice through the implementation of a global community, accountability to God and the people. Jordan also seeks to hold together the impetus toward moderation, civic allegiance, and the radical fulfillment of the human spirit. Turner describes a state of culture that is quixotic, dynamic, and fleeting with the potential to "assuage some of the abrasiveness of the social conflicts rooted in . . . discrepancies in the ordering of social relations."⁵⁶

Jordan's national community combines elements of King's public theology and Turner's dynamic model of community. Perhaps the balance of elements that Jordan seeks can be found in the interstices of theory and praxis, prophetic vision and pragmatic plan. A community of shared interests, mutual respect, and vigorous debate is still not unthinkable. It may be found somewhere between the often harsh realities of human existence and, in Lorraine Hansberry's words, "idyllic possibilities or innocent assessments of the true nature of life."⁵⁷ Jordan raises idyllic and pragmatic possibilities for community life. It is up to future generations to incorporate these possibilities into creative future options.

Chapter 8

Conclusion

The final act in a public drama, whether courtroom, theater, or life, cannot always be predicted. There are twists in the plot, surprise witnesses, or unexpected events. Sometimes without warning there is a sudden ending. Such was the case when Jordan died at fifty-nine years of age. Although she was in poor health for a number of years, her voice seemed to have the staying power to elude the inevitability of death. Like other visionaries of her era (King, the Kennedys, Malcolm, Evers, and others), Jordan left rich but unfinished resources for future generations to consider.

The sudden death of a public person usually inspires admirers to fill with tall tales and fantasy the empty spaces of a life cut short. Ordinary people become mythical giants long before their actual deeds and thoughts move from memory to history. It is hoped that other scholars will examine Jordan's papers and contribute to the understanding of the moral theories of an ordinary black woman who lived life in an extraordinary way.

The speeches reveal a woman who spent a lifetime seeking personal and social equilibrium. Jordan was an articulate woman who eluded many of the cultural snares and indoctrinations imposed by issues of race, class, and gender. Her political acumen helped her to recognize the limitations of essentialist discourse and the potentiality for mainstream backlash. Of more importance, Jordan realized that rigidity is antithetical to human nature. The vicissitudes of life and the pendulum swings of justice guarantee that those who dominate will inevitably give way to the powerless. Even in the most controlled of circumstances, the oppressed sometimes find themselves wielding power. Neither victimization nor villainy is a permanent category. One can reasonably infer from her writings that these realizations led to Jordan's call for education, preparation and fairness. After all, if one cannot predict where the power will lie, one ought to champion justice for all.

Jordan challenged herself and others to live up to a potentially transformative concept of public life. However, her call for a national community was not a position easily assumed. She wrestled with her own understandings of community in North America. She also dealt with the internal conflicts created when her positive self-perceptions collided with negative cultural stereotypes. It must also be noted that when Jordan entered the public sphere, it was bloodied and littered with the ideological remains of visionaries, reactionaries, and a rebellious and vocal generation. Yet she determined that it was better to speak in that arena.

To describe the world that Jordan rhetorically constructed in her speeches is to describe a mediation of differences, a synthesis of interdisciplinary languages, and a resilient optimism. There are few ways to transmit such illusive sentiments without using the incongruities of metaphor, history, drama, and reason. I have argued that Jordan creates a dramatic realm through speeches that integrate ethics, public religion, and law. These three primary themes culminate in her vision of an ideal national community.

At times, Jordan's ethics seem resolute to the point of rigidity. However, her determined moral stance seems to be a corrective to the flaccid shape of public virtue. She believes that the power of virtue to order a society diminishes if moral behavior is not evident in the day-to-day encounters of the citizenry. In that respect, one of the first tenets of her ethics is to behave responsibly toward others. Stories are told of those who met her wrath (however temporary) when they failed to meet this standard. Jordan's eventual disillusionment with politics was related in part to the failure of elected officials to adhere to a consistent policy of ethics in government. Despite her concern with public morality, Jordan does not believe that society has entered a new Dark Age. Instead, she posits the view that virtue can be forgotten or ignored but not eradicated from the human spirit. In her view, provocative speech keeps the idea of community and virtue at the forefront of public discourse.

Jordan's religious inclinations tend toward a mix of black church orthodoxy (Baptist) and public religion. Although she was not known for her religious speeches, her views on religion as a

language of mediation and a facilitator of unity are important contributions to the field. Jordan posits the idea that faith and reason
can be partners in public dialogue. Moreover, she contends that
public service can serve as a productive and relatively untapped
outlet for spiritual activism. Finally, Jordan's religious speeches
chide the black community for its neglect of public policy and
human need. She sees a direct relationship between this neglect and
the demise of strong communal ties.

The legal trajectory in Jordan's speeches wrests law from its
bastions of remote indifference and false neutrality to make it a
practical tool of the people. Jordan is a legal and political pragmatist who describes a national community with both practical
and transcendent elements. Her language posits both the dawn-
ing of moral fulfillment and the practical manifestations of justice
in the lives of ordinary people. As evidenced in the speeches, Jordan's view of justice is an amalgam of many theories. For her,
justice has many facets. It is a virtue, and it is fairness and care.
She gleans these perspectives from philosophers, church folk, and a
close study of the law. Old Testament scholar Walter Brueggemann
summarizes a view of justice that comes very close to Jordan's
practicality. He says justice is "the discernment of what belongs
to whom, and returning it to them."[1] This is a discernment that
relies upon human morality and divine inspiration.

Jordan accomplishes her feats of discernment through proficien-
cies that playwright Eugene O'Neill calls "hopeless hopes ennobled
in art."[2] This remark is not as paradoxical as it seems. O'Neill
says: "Any victory we may win is never the one we dreamed
of winning. Achievement in the narrow sense of possession is a
stale finale."[3] O'Neill puts into words one aspect of Jordan's quest
for mutuality and well-being. To strive for the unattainable is to
"will defeat" and bask in the success of the struggle.[4] The view
of community that Jordan evokes is a rhetorical ideal posited as a
narrative possibility.

Jordan is not alone in her quest for an illusive state of civic
mutuality. The themes of King, Jordan, and Malcolm intersect on
this issue because each of them confronts the dilemma of contested
public turf. If I read Jordan's social theories correctly, her response
to Malcolm's advocacy of separatism focuses on the unavoidable

mutuality inherent in a representative government. That is, that no minority can achieve its goals unless there is some civic or judicial agreement as to the reasonableness of the claims. As sociologist Todd Gitlin concludes, democracy "is a political system of mutual reliance and common moral obligations."[5]

Although Jordan recognizes the value of King's beloved community as a site of moral flourishing and the fulfillment of Christian hope, she seeks more immediate goals. For Jordan, the national community is based on principles enunciated by the nation's founders. As such, the community has identifiable conceptual contours that have not been filled in completely. When Jordan claims civic symbols as the starting point for mutuality, she asks the reader/listener to participate as an extended community of conversant citizens. She also challenges members of dissident groups to recognize the elements of oppression within themselves as well as in others. The ultimate human task is to adjudicate differences without rending the social fabric.[6] In this respect, the search for community is not a naïve quest for unity, but it is, as Jordan states, the search for humanity.

I situate this study of Jordan's speeches amid ongoing discussions about the context and configuration of North American communities in the twenty-first century. As Elizabeth Bounds has argued, the limits of this discussion have not been reached. Bounds correctly describes the history of communitarian rhetoric as "a discourse of lamentation which rewrites liberal optimism and faith in progress as alienation and dissatisfaction."[7] The theme of tragedy and lament is one that Jordan studiously avoids in her early speeches. Somehow she has equated achievement with resolute optimism. This is a choice that muffles the discordant realities of life and adds a tinge of incongruity to some of her pronouncements. When confronted with inconsistencies in some of her views, Jordan retreats to ideal constructs or civic myths. Toward the end of her life, some of the myths were eroding in response to the corrosive effects of an increasing human depravity in public and private lives. War, environmental racism, and resurgent xenophobia caused Jordan to reassess some of her perspectives. Other myths remained intact. Jordan never adjusted her view of the constitutional ideal and the meaning of those precepts for human flourishing, and she never retreated from a belief in the viability of a national community.

In a conversation with Maya Angelou, Jordan said: "There seems to be an overriding presence of evil in the world. It just seems like we are going to be overcome by it. It takes an extraordinary amount of strength to prevail."[8] For Jordan, prevailing meant adding hope to lament in the form of a belief that the shared languages of faith and politics, civic virtue and public service can lead to a renewal of common goals. It also meant projecting the image of a woman-in-control, capable and invulnerable. Part of this image can be attributed to her thunderous voice, and part of the image was donned as she made the treacherous journey from anonymity to public life.

Like Jordan, I have approached this project at the intersection of ethics, public religion, and legal theory. The traditional view of an intersection is that it is a place of convergence and choice. James Gustafson contends that human beings are also intersections where disciplines, arts, and practices meet.[9] When people act as intersections of shared interests for one another, the potential for mutuality increases exponentially and people are freed from the constraints of one-dimensional discourse.

In this regard, I am convinced with Patricia Williams, Mari Matsuda, bell hooks, and others that multiple consciousness has particular relevance for the future study of interpretive discourses; it certainly has particular relevance for the study of Jordan's ideas. In this book, the concepts of multiple consciousness and liminality conjoined to become a vital and dynamic intersection for the consideration of the journey toward moral flourishing. The fluidity of liminality as a discourse and cultural vantage point may help to break the rhetorical impasse between liberals and communitarians.

Communitas is a compelling aspect of a pluralistic community. It nudges the bulwarks of society toward an architectonic reality that remains creative and amenable to change. Although *communitas* evokes elements of risk and precariousness, it also adds a dynamic and life-affirming aspect to the idea of community. As a site of lament and hope, *communitas* urges the "initiate" to embrace the instability of discourse and relationality that undergirds the communities toward which King and Jordan reach.

The themes that I have identified for this analysis do not subsume all of the possibilities for future research. Jordan's personal life, educational perspectives, brief teaching career, and political alliances offer many possibilities for scholarly inquiry. The speeches provide a mere glimpse into the private realms of Jordan's life. Kenneth Burke contends that speeches reveal as much about the speaker as they do about the content of a speech. Jordan's speeches reveal a woman who speaks with an awareness of the human potential for tragedy and hope. In that respect, she reflects her grandfather Patten's training.

I conclude as I began with a story about Patten, a man from whom Jordan gained much of her inner strength. The following excerpt from Jordan's autobiography is worth quoting in full:

> He talked to her as a teacher to a student, as a guide to a traveler, as an aging man to what had become the idol of his life — allowing him to become the foundation, the cornerstone of hers. In time, when she was at college, set on a path of becoming the Washington lawyer of a new generation, he found no further use for himself. One evening drunk on wine, wandering aimlessly, he stumbled on the railroad tracks and was hit by a train, which severed both his legs at the hip.[10]

Patten did not want her to see him in that condition. When she arrived at his hospital bedside, "seeing her one last time, he gave in and died — abdicating a world which had left him without a leg to stand on."[11] This last quotation seems to add a writer's flourish uncharacteristic of the crusty Patten. For he would have known that there is always something to stand on even in the midst of tragedy.

Jordan stood on learned life lessons, family ties, a keen intellect, religious faith, and belief in the potential for human fulfillment. The tragedies were ever present but would not overwhelm Jordan's discourse of hope and possibility. In her speeches, Jordan emerges as a woman who views public life as an opportunity to share the very best that the human spirit can conceive. That is her legacy to ethics, public religion, and law.

Notes

Preface

1. See Barbara Jordan and Shelby Hearon, *Barbara Jordan: A Self-Portrait* (New York: Doubleday & Co., 1979); Ira B. Bryant, *Barbara Charline Jordan: From the Ghetto to the Capitol* (Houston: D. Armstrong Co., 1977); and Mary Beth Rodgers, *Barbara Jordan: American Hero* (New York: Bantam Books, 1998), and James Haskins, *Barbara Jordan* (New York: The Dial Press, 1977).

2. According to Mary Beth Rodgers, Edward A. Patton, Barbara Jordan's great-grandfather, "was one of the last African American Reconstruction politicians to hold public office in Texas" (Rodgers, *American Hero,* 10). The spellings "Patton" and "Patten" both seem to have been used by the family.

3. Jordan was diagnosed with multiple sclerosis in 1973. Eventually she was confined to a wheelchair by a symptom of the disease, distal paresthesia (a weakness of her legs), and other complications (Rodgers, *American Hero,* 198–202).

Chapter 1: Introduction

1. Barbara Jordan, Remarks made to the Women's Day Committee, Metropolitan A.M.E. Zion Church, 14 April 1981, Hartford, Connecticut.

2. James J. Farrell, *The Spirit of the Sixties: The Making of Postwar Radicalism* (New York: Routledge, 1997), 137–201.

3. Jordan, "Equality, Liberty and the Pursuit of Community in America." Remarks before the Texas Committee for the Humanities, 13 November 1987, University of Texas School of Law, Austin, Texas.

4. To date, only a few of Jordan's political speeches have been analyzed. See Donald R. Martin and Vickey G. Martin, "Barbara Jordan's Symbolic Use of Language in the Keynote Address to the National Women's Conference," *The Southern Speech Communication Journal* 49 Spring (1984): 319–33; Wayne N. Thompson, "Barbara Jordan's Keynote Address: Fulfilling Dual and Conflicting Purposes," *Central States Speech Journal* 30 Fall (1979): 273–77; Barbara Jordan Commemorative Issue, 5 Texas J. Women & L. (1996).

5. Elizabeth Bounds discusses in detail the "concerted liberal effort throughout the 1950s and 1960s to present a linear and unified view of

the world." *Coming Together/Coming Apart: Religion, Community and Modernity* (New York and London: Routledge, 1997), 35.

6. Howard Harrod, *The Human Center: Moral Agency in the Social World* (Philadelphia: Fortress Press, 1981), 44.

7. See Theodore Turnau's discussion of principled pluralism in "Speaking in Broken Tongue: Postmodernism, Principled Pluralism and the Rehabilitation of Public Moral Discourse," *Westminster Theological Journal* 56 (1994): 345–77. Turnau argues that consensus requires the recognition that pluralism rests on principles and values that transcend difference. He distinguishes between different types of pluralism. Pan-Protestant pluralism is the legacy of Congregational Puritanism. It emphasizes the completeness of an individual without reference to an originating group. European traditional pluralism emphasizes the necessity of an individual's identification with a group, wherever American pluralism takes the liberal idea of personal autonomy to isolationist extremes. See also Darryl Baskin, "The Congregational Origins of American Pluralism," *Journal of Church and State* 11 (1969): 277–80, 353–57. Jordan's ideas about pluralism assume that those engaged in the social enterprise will contribute to its success through their public service, responsibility, and faith in the civic narrative.

8. Because Jordan assumes a broad base of shared values, her references to specific values are exemplary and not exhaustive. She also identifies equality, liberty, freedom, justice, independence, respect for others, and opportunity as "core, central, foundation values." Jordan, "A Wake-up Call for the American Dream." Remarks given to Project ACHIEVE, 6 December 1990, Northside High School, Memphis, Tennessee.

9. Because the thesis of this book relies on a unified reading of Jordan's speeches, chapter headings used to organize the discussion of ethics, public religion, and law should not be considered rigid analytical categories. The synthesis of themes in the speeches would render such an approach untenable.

10. Jordan, "The Church and Public Policy," National Religious Liberty Conference, 7 October 1986, First Baptist Church, Washington, D.C. Jordan's discussion of the separation of church and state is gleaned from various sources including: Thomas Jefferson's Letter to the Baptists of Danbury, Roger Williams (The Howe Lectures), and Justice Hugo Black's opinion in *Everson v. Board of Education*, 330 U.S. 1, 16 (1947). Justice Black wrote: "The First Amendment has erected a wall between church and state. That wall must be kept high and impregnable. We could not approve the slightest breach." See also Ronald F. Thiemann, *Religion in Public Life: A Dilemma for Democracy* (Washington, D.C.: Georgetown University Press, 1996), 42–66.

11. Jordan, "Is Ethics a Component of Government?" Remarks made at

the University of California at Santa Barbara, 22 September 1990, Santa Barbara, California.

12. Molly Ivins, "The First and Only," Transcript of an interview with Charlayne Hunter-Gault after Jordan's death. *The NewsHour,* 17 January 1996.

13. Robert L. Scott and James W. Chesebro, eds., *Methods of Rhetorical Criticism: A Twentieth Century Perspective,* 3d ed. (Detroit: Wayne State University Press, 1990), 16.

14. Kenneth Burke, *A Rhetoric of Motives* (Berkeley: University of California Press, 1969), 41; and *The Philosophy of Literary Form* (New York: Random House, 1957), 3. Burke, a prolific self-educated writer and theorist, was born in 1897 and died in 1995. In the 1960s, Burke's dramatistic theory decentered the traditional rhetorical focus and exponentially expanded a limited field of critical inquiry.

15. Bruce E. Gronbeck, "Dramaturgical Theory and Criticism: The State of the Art (or Science?)," *The Western Journal of Speech Communication,* 44 (Fall 1980): 315–30. Because human conduct is a series of dramatic fulfillments and failures, Burke believes that human relations and motives are best revealed by using the formal art of drama and applying those lessons to the informal art of living. Speeches become rhetorical minidramas with words acting as protagonists.

16. Harold J. Berman, *Faith and Order: The Reconciliation of Law and Religion* (Atlanta: Scholars Press, 1993), 10.

17. Denise Brissett and Charles Edgley, eds., "The Dramaturgical Perspective," *Life as Theatre,* 2d ed. (New York: Aldine de Gruyter, 1990, x.

18. Kenneth Burke, *Permanence and Change and Attitudes Toward History,* 3d ed. (Berkeley: University of California Press, 1984), 119. See also "Twelve Propositions," 21. Burke commends the controversial use of fragmentary and tentative conclusions in rhetorical analysis. He is not a proponent of sloppy scholarship; he is proposing a generative analysis — a type of interpretive risk-taking intrinsic to drama.

19. A full discussion of Turner's theories and their relevance to Jordan's speeches can be found in chapters 2 and 7. The word *liminality* comes from the Latin word *limen,* or threshold, and denotes the transition from one culturally defined state or status to another. Turner notes that a liminal space "is a very long threshold, a corridor almost, or a tunnel which may become a pilgrim's road, or, passing from dynamics to statics, may cease to be a mere transition and become a set way of life." The term *communitas* refers to the emergence of an immediate and spontaneous communal event that is dramatic, performative, and transitory. See Victor Turner, *Blazing the Trail: Way Marks in the Exploration of Symbols,* ed. Edith Turner (Tucson and London: University of Arizona Press, 1992), 49.

20. Michael Lind, "Jordan's Rules," *The New Republic,* 12 February 1996.

Chapter 2: Other Expectations

1. Jordan and Hearon, *Barbara Jordan*, 2.
2. Ibid.
3. Ibid., 118. Angela D. Gilmore also makes reference to the "box" of silence that held her captive while she attempted to integrate herself into an antagonistic society. Jordan, Gilmore, and Lorde come to the conclusion that despite the risks, it is better to speak. Gilmore, "It Is Better to Speak," 6 Berkeley Women's L.J. (1990–91): 74, 80.
4. Ibid., 5, 9.
5. Ibid., 10. In her autobiography, Jordan says that she never knew the source of this quotation.
6. Ibid., 7.
7. 163 U.S. 537, 544, 1896. The *Plessy* case involved a person deemed to be 7/8 Caucasian who was jailed for sitting in a whites-only railroad coach in Louisiana. The Supreme Court rendered the opinion that the separation of the races in places where they were liable to come into contact did not necessarily imply the inferiority of either race. *Plessy* was overruled in *Brown v. Board of Education* 347 U.S. 483 (1854).
8. Gay Elliott McFarland, "Barbara Jordan's Houston," *Houston Chronicle*, 5 February, 1979, Sec. 2.
9. Jordan and Hearon, *Barbara Jordan*, 62.
10. bell hooks, *Yearning: Race, Gender and Cultural Politics* (Boston: South End Press, 1990), 113. See also Victor Anderson's discussion of the ontological blackness that whiteness created in *Beyond Ontological Blackness* (New York: Continuum Press, 1995).
11. Molly Ivins, "She Sounded Like God," *The New York Times Magazine*, 29 December, 1996.
12. *Texas Observer*, Austin, Texas, November 1972.
13. Molly Ivins, "Barbara Jordan's Freedom Medal Shows Our Progress," *Houston Post*, 10 August, 1994, Sec. 21.
14. See Cornel West's discussion of nihilism in *Race Matters* (New York: Viking Books, 1993).
15. Audre Lorde, *Sister Outsider: Essays and Speeches by Audre Lorde* (Trumansburg, N.Y.: The Crossing Press, 1984) 152, 156.
16. bell hooks, *Picturing Us*, ed. Deborah Willis (New York: The New Press, 1994), 84.
17. Jordan, Remarks made at the University of Missouri, *Missouri Magazine* awards for Public Service, 1 November 1977, New York.
18. Bryant, *Barbara Charline Jordan*, 20. Bryant's conclusion is interesting but can't be verified. It is just as likely that she simply developed into a fully-figured woman.
19. Jordan and Hearon, *Barbara Jordan*, 7.
20. Ibid., 18–20. Jordan's grandfather armed himself and attempted to apprehend a thief who had stolen merchandise from his store. A police

officer opened fire when he saw a "negro with a gun." Patten raised his hands to surrender, but was shot. He returned fire before he realized that he was in a gun battle with a white police officer. No one was killed, but Patten was convicted of assault with intent to murder, by an all-white jury. He was sentenced to ten years, but was pardoned some years later.

21. "Jordan Chides Bush's Frequent Misstatements," *Houston Post,* 1 October 1988, Sec. A-1.

22. Kathy Kiely, "Jordan Gets Heat for Job Registry Plan," *Houston Post,* 7 August 1994, Sec. A-25.

23. Jordan, Handwritten memo quoting Edgar Snow's *Journey to the Beginning* (New York: Random House, 1958). Jordan frequently referred to this excerpt from Snow's book: "I want nothing to do with any religion concerned with keeping the masses satisfied to live in human filth and ignorance. I want nothing to do with any order, religious or otherwise, which does not teach people that they are capable of becoming happier and more civilized on this earth, capable of becoming true man, master of his fate and captain of his soul."

24. I use the term *spokesperson* with some caution as Jordan is uncomfortable with the label. She says in the speech "Who Speaks for the Negro?:" "No one [speaks for the Negro], his[her] presence speaks for itself." Remarks given at a conference entitled "The Role of the News Media and Race Relations," 27 May 1968, Austin, Texas, p. 15. Handwritten speech, Robert J. Terry (RJT) Archives, Houston, Texas.

25. Victor Turner, *The Ritual Process: Structure and Anti-Structure* (Chicago: University of Chicago Press, 1969), 95.

26. Ibid., 97.

27. Hans Blumenberg, *The Legitimacy of the Modern Age* (Boston: MIT Press, 1983), 64.

28. Jordan and Hearon, *Barbara Jordan,* 1.

29. Turner, *Ritual Process,* 94.

30. Burke's dramatistic methodology requires an examination of the rhetorical agent's response to relevant social factors such as hierarchy, dominance, and control.

31. Jordan and Hearon, *Barbara Jordan,* 115, quoting Rice University professor Richard Murray, who acted as a consultant to her first campaign. See also Rodgers, *American Hero,* 89.

32. Ibid., 116.

33. Jacqueline Jones Royster offers a similar analysis in "To Call a Thing by Its True Name: The Rhetoric of Ida B. Wells," *Reclaiming Rhetorica,* ed. Andrea Lundsford (Pittsburgh and London: University of Pittsburgh Press, 1995), 171–75.

34. Audre Lorde, "A Litany for Survival," *The Black Unicorn* (New York: W. W. Norton Co., 1978), 32.

35. Ibid., 31.

36. In Kwesi Yankah's book *Speaking for the Chief: Okyeame and the Politics of Akan Royal Oratory* (Bloomington and Indianapolis: Indiana University Press, 1995). Yankah discusses the limits of feminine public discourse in West Africa and the creative alternatives developed as a result of their exclusion. Those alternatives include textile messages and proverbial sayings embossed or batiked on their clothing.

37. Drema Libscomb, "Sojourner Truth: A Practical Public Discourse," ed. Andrea Lundsford, *Reclaiming Rhetorica*, 227–45.

38. Royster, "To Call a Thing by Its True Name," 167–201.

39. Michael Lind, "Jordan's Rules," *The New Republic*. Though few would admit it even now, the desire to assimilate was so great that some during Jordan's era considered it a compliment to be mistaken for a European-American on the telephone.

40. The black club women's movement developed between 1892 and 1894. For a view of this social movement as a mediator of interstructured oppression, see Marcia Riggs's discussion in *Awake Arise and Act: A Womanist Call for Black Liberation* (Cleveland: Pilgrim Press, 1995), 82–87.

41. Cornel West also discusses this issue in *Keeping Faith: Philosophy and Race in America* (New York: Routledge, 1993).

42. Jordan, "Remarks," *Missouri Magazine*, p. 8.

43. The mirror metaphor is adopted from Hauerwas's discussion of the Christian community. He contends that it should be a mirror to the world in need of its gifts. See *The Peaceable Kingdom* (Notre Dame: University of Notre Dame Press, 1983), 15.

44. Jordan's refusal to allow intrusions into her personal life led to much speculation about her health and her sexuality. Other than an unsubstantiated report by the *Gay Advocate* I found no data that would support the innuendo. After her death, her roommate Nancy Earl said simply, "I was her good friend. I was there morning and night to help her get up and get showered and get dressed and go to work. She had lots of companions. People can say whatever they want. She was a friend of mine." Barbara Jordan, "The Other Life," *Gay Advocate*, 6 March 1996. As her health declined, Jordan often had health workers help her with her personal care. Jordan's health problems were extensive and required the aid and assistance of her friends. Any conclusion beyond Earl's comments and Jordan's silence would be highly speculative.

Chapter 3: The Speeches in Historical Context

1. Jordan, "American Imports Revalued: Tributaries of American Culture." Lecture given on 25 July 1976, Ditchley Foundation, Ditchley Park, Oxfordshire, England.

2. "The Times They Are A-Changin'." Words and Music by Bob Dylan, © 1963, 1964, by Warner Bros. Inc., Copyright renewed 1991 by Special Rider Music. Used by permission.

3. Theologian James Lawson's conversation with the author. Here, I am, quoting his salient assessment of the effects of the Civil Rights movement. February 1999, Memphis Theological Seminary, Memphis, Tennessee.

4. Historian Lewis Baldwin argues that King failed to realize that his dream of integration was no more realistic than Garvey's or Malcolm X's call for separation. *To Make the Wounded Whole* (Minneapolis: Fortress Press, 1992), 24.

5. Martin's and Malcolm's goals should not be perceived as irreconcilable. See Dr. King's discussion of black power before the Rabbinical Assembly, 25 March 1968. *A Testament of Hope: The Essential Writings and Speeches of Martin Luther King Jr.*, ed. James M. Washington (San Francisco: HarperSanFrancisco, 1986).

6. Jordan, "The Idea of Civil Rights."

7. Jordan, "The Great Society: A Twenty-Year Critique." Remarks at a symposium sponsored by the L. B. J. Library and the L. B. J. School of Public Affairs, April 1985, Austin, Texas.

8. See Roger Lundin's treatment of historical memory, faith, and realism in *Disciplining Hermeneutics: Interpretation in Christian Perspectives* (Grand Rapid, Mich.: Wm. B. Eerdmans, 1997), 25–47.

9. Richard Sennett, "The Rhetoric of Ethnic Identity," *The End of Rhetoric: History, Theory, Practice,* eds. John Bender and David E. Wellbery (Stanford: Stanford University Press, 1990), 191–206.

10. Ibid., 200. According to Sennett, historical events become stories that allow issues of identity to be creatively redacted. However, when Sennett talks of ethnic identity, he emphasizes the negative effects of "outsider politics" without acknowledging the positive self-sustaining elements developed by rejected groups. Others have made the same mistake. In the push toward integration, African American leaders, including Martin Luther King Jr., lost sight of the moral strength and vigor of their own community. Jordan emphasizes those strengths and urges their retention. She is aware that her skills were recognized and nurtured first in the black community. However, she also realizes that race does not subsume the entire field of moral discourse.

11. Jordan, "A Wake-up Call for the American Dream." Remarks given to Project ACHIEVE, 6 December 1990, Northside High School, Memphis, Tennessee.

12. Ibid.

13. Ibid.

14. Jordan, "Who Speaks for the Negro?"

15. Reinhold Niebuhr, "The Sin of Racial Prejudice," *The Messenger* 13: 6, 3 February 1948.

16. Jordan, "Who Speaks for the Negro?"

17. This broader concern is evidenced in her attempts to broaden the scope of the 1964 Civil Rights Act, which originally prohibited discrimination in federally assisted programs on the basis of race, color, or national origin. Jordan expands coverage to sex, age, and handicap.

18. I chose Baldwin as a counterpoint to Jordan's theories because they addressed the same issues from different rhetorical perspectives. Jordan was considered a black conservative, who was occasionally accused of being co-opted by the political interests of her party and the majority culture. Baldwin was the "bad boy" of literature and cultural criticism.

19. Sennett, "Rhetoric of Ethnic Identity," 191–206.

20. James Baldwin, *The Fire Next Time: My Dungeon Shook* (New York: The Dial Press, 1963), originally published as "Letter to My Nephew," *The Progressive* (1962).

21. Jordan, "Who Speaks for the Negro?"

22. Ibid.

23. Jordan, "The New Discrimination." Handwritten speech, n.d., pp. 8, 9, RJT Archives, Houston, Texas.

24. Ibid.

25. Jordan, "The Idea of Civil Rights," 2.

26. Jordan, Address to Concerned and Caring Educators, Omaha, Nebraska, 22 February, 1992.

27. James Baldwin, *The Price of the Ticket*, 663.

28. During a symposium celebrating the twentieth anniversary of the Great Society, panel members identify the gap between speech and action that persists in the public sector.

29. Lyndon Baines Johnson, untitled remarks given at the University of Michigan, 2 May 1964.

30. "Lyndon Johnson and the Concept of Equal Basic Liberty or the Political Stirrings of An Uncommon Texan." Keynote address given at Hofstra University, 10 April 1986.

31. It is interesting to note that Jordan recounts Johnson's unknown acts of conscience, which all occur many decades before his presidency: in 1957, Johnson became the first Texas senator since 1875 to vote for a Civil Rights bill; he backed Adlai Stevenson for president despite Stevenson's unpopular position on federal ownership of Texan tidelands; and Johnson intervened in 1949 on behalf of a Mexican soldier killed in WW II. The soldier was denied official funeral services because of his ethnicity. Jordan, Keynote Address, 10 April 1986, pp. 1–2, at Hofstra University.

32. Ibid., 1.

33. Ibid., 4. The biblical quotation makes reference to Isaiah 1:18.

34. See Cornel West's discussion of prophetic language in *Prophetic*

Fragments: Illumination of the Crisis in American Religion and Culture (Grand Rapids, Mich.: Wm. B. Eerdmans, 1988).

35. Jordan, "Looking for a Vision of the 1990s," Great Society Round-up, 5 May 1990, RJT Archives, Houston, Texas.

36. Ibid., 2.

37. Jordan, "Remarks, Susan B. Anthony Annual Banquet," 10 November 1973, quoting Lyndon Johnson's remarks at the University of Michigan, n.d., Houston, Texas, reprinted in 5 Texas J. Women & L. (1996): 245–47.

Chapter 4: Ethics: Here Be Dragons

1. Jordan, "In Search of Humanity." Remarks at fund-raising banquet, 19 October 1974, reprinted in 5 Texas J. Women & L. (1995): 181–85.

2. Baldwin makes these observations in the context of an article that considers androgyny in America as a metaphor for human unity. *The Price of the Ticket,* 679.

3. Hans Küng raises similar questions in an international context in *Global Responsibility: In Search of a New World Ethic* (New York: Continuum Press), 1993.

4. Ann Stuhldreher, "Listen to that Still, Small Voice," *The New Texas Agenda: The Governor's Appointee Newsletter.* Barbara Jordan's response to an interviewer when she was acting as special ethics adviser to Governor Ann Richards, Office of the Governor, Austin, Texas (Summer 1994), p. 3.

5. Jordan, Remarks before the Public Broadcasting System Program Fair Banquet, 6 November 1986, Hyatt Regency Hotel, Austin, Texas.

6. Don Kerr, "Jordan: Ethical Servants Need Moral Qualities," *Houston Chronicle,* n.d., Houston, Texas.

7. Professors Thonssen and Baird contend that "rhetoric, as the intermediary between the will to action and the achievement of the result, must accordingly be conceived as both a political and an ethical instrument." However, it should not be assumed that this synergy alludes to a necessary relationship between any of the derivative contexts or themes in Jordan's speeches. Sometimes they are congruent, at other times the conflict is apparent. Jordan allows the tributaries of politics, religion, and ethics to jostle for primacy in her speeches to enhance the interpretive framework. Lester Thonssen and A. Craig Baird, *Speech Criticism* (New York: The Ronald Press Co., 1948), 467.

8. Victor Anderson, "The Question of Ethics, Indeed!" Unpublished paper p. 8, Vanderbilt University, Nashville, Tennessee.

9. Michel Maffesoli argues that an ethic of the everyday cannot exclude collective emotions, feelings, and customs. See *The Time of the Tribes: The Decline of Individualism in Mass Society,* trans. Don Smith (London: Sage Publications, 1996).

10. Anderson, "Indeed," 7.

11. See Bob Woodward's discussion of the extended ramifications of Watergate on the politics of the nation in *Shadow: Five Presidents and the Legacy of Watergate* (New York: Simon Schuster, 1999).

12. Jordan, "In Search of Humanity." Remarks at fund-raising banquet, 19 October 1974, reprinted in 5 Texas J. Women & L. (1995): 181–85.

13. Maffesoli, *Tribes*, 11.

14. Jordan, "Opening Statement to the House Judiciary Committee Proceedings on Impeachment of Richard Nixon," 93d Cong. 2d Sess. 111, Washington, D.C., 25 July 1974.

15. The pentad is a structural model used to describe the act (what was done), scene (when or where it occurred), agent (who did it), agency (how it was done), and the purpose of the speech. Use of Burke's five categories facilitates the descriptive process in rhetorical analysis by determining the dominant rhetorical clusters. The result is that a particular emphasis emerges: the speaker, her context, or the ends-means ratio.

16. Jordan's emphasis on the historical race-based exclusion of African Americans from the 1787 Preamble to the Constitution indicates that this is not going to be the usual speech of a veteran Washingtonian with political baggage. After the hearing, Jordan would put the entire pre-impeachment proceedings in a different light. Declining to discuss what her vote would have been, she says, "I don't feel that black people have become too focused on the matter of impeachment. Whether Richard Nixon is in office or out, you are still going to be black." "Representative Barbara Jordan Denies Talk with Rodino," *Houston Chronicle*, 8 July 1974, p. 11, sec. 1.

17. Jordan, "Impeachment speech."

18. Jordan, "Women and the Constitution: The Challenge." Remarks 11 February 1988, Atlanta, Georgia.

19. *Dred Scott v. Sandford*, 60 U.S. 393, 405, 407–8 (1857).

20. A word about the proverbial "we" used so frequently in Jordan's speeches. Maffesoli (Tribes, 12) refers to the aesthetic of "we" as "a mixture of indifference and periodic bursts of energy." It is a rhetorical cleaving and rending of the social order. According to Maffesoli's criteria, " 'We' can be a combination of things that don't necessarily belong together, or nexus — the melding of things that are integral to one another." In my view Jordan's speeches model another view of the collective "we." Her speeches connect disparate elements while allowing moral particularisms to remain distinct.

21. The penumbra doctrine refers to the implied powers of the federal government regarding issues such as privacy. The doctrine is predicated on the Necessary and Proper Clause of the U.S. Constitution, Art. I, Sec. 8 (18), which allows one implied power to be engrafted onto another implied power. *Kohl v. U.S.*, 91 U.S. 367, 23 L. Ed. 449.

22. Jordan, "In Search of Humanity."

23. See Donald and Vickey Martin's discussion of Jordan's symbolic use of shared meaning in "Symbolic Use," 324–27.

24. Jordan, "Moving on from Watergate." Remarks given at the Texas Law Review Annual Banquet, 8 March 1975, Driskoll Hotel, Austin, Texas. In this speech, Jordan says that she is unwilling to use the Watergate case as a "model of evil," when the tape erasures, bungling burglars, and despotic fumblings of the president resemble more closely a comic opera. In every drama, there is a thin line between catastrophe and hilarity.

25. Ibid.

26. Jordan, "We Can't Legislate Happiness," 4.

27. Jordan, "Conviction Values." Commencement address at the University of Texas, 24 May 1986, Houston, Texas.

28. Küng, *Global Responsibility.*

29. Jordan and Rostow, *The Great Society: A Twenty-Year Critique* (Lyndon B. Johnson School of Public Affairs Publications, 1986), 7.

30. For further discussions of applied moral norms, *Ethics and the Moral Life* (London: Macmillan, 1958).

31. Jordan makes reference to the work of Reinhold Niebuhr in *Moral Man and Immoral Society: A Study in Ethics and Politics* (1st ed. New York: C. Scribner's Sons, 1932; 2d ed. New York: Scribner, 1960). Jordan summarizes his argument in the following way: The highest ideal for the society is justice, and the highest ideal for the individual is selflessness. Because neither is attainable, the remaining option is peaceful coexistence. Jordan argues that although pure selflessness may be an impossible goal, enlightened self-interest is not.

32. Jordan, "The Universalization of the Philosophy or Ethic of Responsibility." Commencement address at the University of Louisville Law School, 15 May 1994, Louisville, Kentucky.

33. Alasdair MacIntyre correctly identifies historical differences in the ordering of values, offering a few examples of the differences between the values of Homer, Aristotle, and the New Testament. Ultimately, McIntyre recognizes core concepts in the values of varied traditions. *After Virtue*, 2d ed. (Notre Dame: University of Notre Dame Press, 1984).

34. Jordan, "Conviction Values," 2.

35. Ibid.

36. Jordan, "Values in Common." Commencement address at Middlebury College, 24 May 1987, Middlebury, Vermont.

37. Ibid., 4.

38. Coincidentally, Jordan's two convention speeches preceded two Democratic wins: Jimmy Carter in 1976 and Bill Clinton in 1992. See also Mary Beth Rodgers, "Barbara Jordan's Influence on the Democratic Party Reflected in Two Keynote Addresses to National Party Conventions," 5 Texas J. Women & L. (1996): 185.

39. The phrase "deferred dreams" is taken from Langston Hughes, *Collected Poems* (New York: Alfred A. Knopf, 1994).

40. Thompson, "Barbara Jordan's Keynote Address."

41. Jordan, "Who Then Will Speak for the Common Good?" Democratic Convention Keynote Address, 12 July 1976, New York.

42. Thompson, "Keynote," 277.

43. Jordan, "Change: From What to What?" Democratic Convention Keynote Address, 13 July 1992, New York.

44. Ibid.

45. Jordan, "Change," 1.

46. Michael J. Perry, "Is the Idea of Human Rights Ineliminably Religious?" 27 U. Rich. L. Rev. (1993): 1023–81.

47. From *Collected Poems* by Langston Hughes. Copyright © 1994 by the Estate of Langston Hughes. Reprinted by permission of Alfred A. Knopf, a Division of Random House, Inc.

48. John Finnis, *Natural Law, Natural Rights* (Oxford: Clarendon Press 1980), 14.

49. Here Jordan makes reference to Reinhold Niebuhr's theory.

50. Jordan, "The Common Good: A Framework for Discussion and Consensus." Remarks at the Southwest meeting of the American Assembly at the LBJ Library, 11 May 1990, Austin, Texas.

51. Jordan, "Who Then Will Speak," 2.

52. Ibid.

53. Ibid 3.

54. Ibid.

55. Jordan, "Common Good" 1.

56. Ibid., 2, 3.

57. Jordan, "Compassion v. Tough Love or Mother Teresa v. Marie Antoinette." Remarks at the Federation for Community Planning, Cleveland, Ohio, 20 March 1992, 1.

58. Ibid.

59. Ibid., 3.

60. Ibid.

61. William Dean, *The Religious Critic in American Culture* (New York: State University of New York, 1994), xix.

62. Robert Bellah, *The Broken Covenant: American Civil Religion in Time of Trial* (Chicago: University of Chicago Press, 1993).

63. Jordan, "How Do We Live with Each Other's Deepest Differences?" 2, quoting the Williamsburg Charter.

64. Ibid.

65. Burke's discursive pairings "us-them" are analyzed in Timothy W. Cursius's "Burke's Dialectic and Rhetoric," *Philosophy and Rhetoric* (1986): 29. Discursive pairings assume the contradictory influences of antithesis, enmity, and resolution. The hope of consubstantiality lies in

the healing of radical divisions through the sifting of incommensurate languages.

66. The melting pot is a mold that did not affect some ethnic groups. Thurgood Marshall in a characteristically pithy comment once remarked that "if America is a melting pot, the Negro either did not get into the pot or it didn't melt down." Jordan quoting Marshall, "E Pluribus Unum," 4.

67. Israel Zangwill, *The Melting Pot* (1909). The original theme of the play was intermarriage between immigrants. It seems that the more colorful and xenophobic depictions of the melting pot transformations occurred in later adaptations. By 1916, the Ford Motor Company English School was using Zangwill's play with those added flourishes. Zangwill did not coin the term "melting pot." The idea can be traced to the eighteenth century. Emerson and Theodore Roosevelt also evoked the image. For further information see Harley Erdman, *Staging the Jew: The Performance of an American Ethnicity 1860–1920* (New York: Rutgers University Press, 1997), 134–39.

68. Jordan, Remarks to the Immigration and Naturalization Service, INS Commissioner's Conference, 28 November 1995, Philadelphia, Pennsylvania, 6.

69. Bernhard Waldenfels, "The Other and the Foreign," *Philosophy and Social Criticism* 21. no. 5/6 (Sept./Nov. 1995).

70. Georgia Anne Geyer, "Thanks, Barbara Jordan: Let's Get that I.D. Card," Universal Press Syndicate, n.d.; Tess Borden, "Registry Would Slow Illegals, Jordan Says," *Houston Post*, 12 October 1994; Mike Tolson, "Jordan Makes Pitch for Immigration Plan," *Houston Chronicle*, 12 October 1994, p. 18A.

71. Abraham Joshua Heschel, *I Asked for Wonder: A Spiritual Anthology* (New York: Crossroad, 1991), 52.

72. Dana Wilbanks, "The Moral Debate Between Humanitarianism and National Interest About U.S. Refugee Policy: A Theological Perspective," *Migration World* 21, No. 5: 15–18.

73. Baldwin, *Price of the Ticket,* 690.

74. Jordan, "Deepest Differences," 7.

Chapter 5: Religion in the Public Sphere

1. Jordan, "The Role and Concern of Christian Women in Politics," 4, RJT Archives, Houston, Texas.

2. Heschel, *Wonder,* 41

3. I am grateful for conversations with the late Dr. Lucy Rose about the harshness of light and the respite of darkness. Columbia Theological Seminary, Fall 1995, Atlanta, Georgia.

4. Jordan, Remarks, Metropolitan A.M.E. Zion Church.

5. Heschel, *Wonder,* 57.

6. Jordan and Hearon, *Barbara Jordan,* 96, 97.

7. Ibid.

8. Archie Epps, *Malcolm X: Speeches at Harvard* (New York: Paragon House, 1991), 115–31; James Cone, *Black Theology and Black Power* (San Francisco: Harper & Row 1989); J. Deotis Roberts, *Liberation and Reconciliation: A Black Theology* (Philadelphia, Westminster Press, 1971).

9. Exodus 34:29–35.

10. 1 Chronicles 13:10.

11. Jordan, "Mankind: The Meeting Place of Church and State," Charles P. Taft Memorial Lecture, 28 April 1988, Christ Church, Cincinnati, Ohio.

12. bell hooks, "Feet of the Messenger: Remembering Malcolm X," *Yearning,* 79–88, 81, quoting *The Autobiography of Malcolm X* (New York: Grove Press, 1965).

13. Ibid., 83.

14. Jordan, "The Church and Public Policy," National Religious Liberty Conference, 7 October 1986, Washington, D.C.

15. Rudolf Otto, *The Idea of the Holy: An Inquiry into the Non-Rational Factor in the Idea of the Divine and Its Relation to the Rational,* trans. John W. Harvey (Oxford: Oxford University Press, 1923, 1950).

16. Ibid., 27.

17. Perry, "Human Rights," 1061.

18. Jordan, Remarks, Metropolitan A.M.E. Zion Church.

19. Ibid.

20. Linell E. Cady, *Religion, Theology, and American Public Life* (Albany: State University of New York Press, 1993), 6–29.

21. Jordan, "Meeting Place," 2.

22. In her speech entitled "The Church and Public Policy," Jordan makes reference to Thomas Jefferson's discussion of the separation of church and state in his letter to the Baptists of Danbury, Connecticut. He says, "I contemplate with sovereign reverence...that act of the whole American people which declared that their legislature should 'make no law respecting an establishment of religion or prohibiting the free exercise thereof,' thus building a wall of separation between church and state."

23. Jordan, "Meeting Place."

24. Ibid.

25. Cady, *Public Life,* 11–13.

26. Ibid., 23.

27. José Casanova, *Public Religions in the Modern World* (Chicago: University of Chicago Press, 1994).

28. Jordan, Remarks, Metropolitan A.M.E. Zion Church.

29. Ibid.

30. Jordan, "Christian Women in Politics, 5."

31. Ibid., 4.

32. Cady, *Public Life.*

33. Jordan, "Prayer of Representative Jordan at the National Prayer Breakfast," 2 February 1978, Washington, D.C.

34. Ibid.

35. Jordan, "The Church and Public Policy," 4, 6.

36. Jordan, "Barriers to Wholeness," 4, 14 March 1987, United Church of Christ, New Orleans.

37. Jordan, "Women in Action: Religious, Responsible Role Models," p. 2. Remarks given on Women's Day, 24 April 1994, Good Hope Missionary Baptist Church, Houston, Texas.

38. Ibid., 3, 4.

39. Ibid., 2.

40. Ibid., 3, 4.

41. Andrew King, "The Rhetorical Legacy of the Black Church," *The Central States Speech Journal,* 22, no. 1 (Spring 1971): 179.

42. W. E. B. Du Bois, *The Souls of Black Folk* (Greenwich, Conn.: Fawcett Publishers, 1901, 1961), 146.

43. James Baldwin, *Notes of a Native Son* (Boston: Beacon Press, 1955), 66.

44. Joseph R. Washington, *Black Religion: The Negro's Church in the United States* (Boston: Beacon Press, 1964); Benjamin Mays and Joseph Nicholson, *The Negro Church* (New York: Institute of Social and Religious Research, 1933), 91.

45. Jordan, "Christian Women in Politics," 6.

46. Jordan, "Barriers to Wholeness," 5.

47. Ibid.

48. Ibid.

49. Ibid.

50. Ibid., 7.

51. Jordan, "Barriers to Wholeness," 7.

52. Jordan, "Christian Women in Politics," 5, 6.

53. See Hans-Georg Gadamer, *The Philosophy of Hans-George Gadamer,* ed. Lewis Edwin Han, Library of Living Philosophers, Vol. 24 (Carbondale, Ill.: Open Court Publishing Co., 1997).

54. Jordan, "Barriers to Wholeness," 2.

55. Ibid.

56. Ibid., 5.

Chapter 6: Law: Against the Prevailing Wind

1. Barbara Jordan and Elspeth D. Rostow, eds., "The Great Society and Its Markings," *The Great Society: A Twenty-Year Critique* (Austin: University of Texas Press, 1986), 7.

2. Carl T. Rowan, *Dream Makers, Dream Breakers: The Word of Justice Thurgood Marshall* (Boston: Little, Brown & Co., 1993), 453–54. See also Derrick Bell, "Thurgood Marshall," 69 N.Y.U. L. Rev. (1994): See also Wendy Brown-Scott, "Justice Thurgood Marshall and the Integrative Ideal" 26 Ariz. St. L.J. (Summer 1994): 535–60.

3. Brown-Scott, "Justice Thurgood Marshall."

4. Cornelius F. Murphy, Jr., *Modern Legal Philosophy* (Pittsburgh: Duquesne University Press, 1978).

5. Catherine McKinnon, "Toward Feminist Jurisprudence," *Feminist Jurisprudence* (New York and London: Oxford University Press, 1993), 610.

6. See the *Constitutional Commentary* 8, no. 2 (Summer): 349. Legal theorist J. M. Balkin offers "The Top Ten Reasons to Be a Legal Pragmatist." In a humorous vein, he suggests that "it works; being a legal pragmatist means never having to say you have a theory. You can also be a civic republican, [a] feminist, a deconstructionist, a case-cruncher . . . a law economics type, or anything else." These are pretty broad parameters, but Jordan narrows the scope of her concerns. She considers law a necessary interpretive element in her construals of ethics and public religion. Moreover, she considers the discursive interplay between these three categories crucial to a redemption of shared values.

7. "Holmes and the Pragmatists," 41 Stan. L. Rev. 787, 864–70, quoting R. Perry, 459–61, 1 Holmes-Pollock Letters dated June 17, 1908. Although Holmes is considered a pragmatist by most, a review of his letters indicates some ambivalence about the theory. Among other statements, he is quoted as saying, "I think pragmatism an amusing humbug." This private opinion does not diminish his writings on the subject.

8. Mari J. Matsuda, "Pragmatism Modified and the False Consciousness Problem," 63 So. Calif. L. Rev. (1990): 1763–82.

9. Cornel West, "The Limits of NeoPragmatism," 63 So. Calif. L. Rev. (1990): 1747–51.

10. Ibid.

11. Natural law legal theorists hold the theory that there is an affinity between law and morality. Positivists hold the view that there is no necessary connection. The use of the term "natural law in legal theory" should not be confused with the term "natural law in moral theory." In a moral context, the term refers to the objective status of moral norms. Natural law in legal terms has roots in the Greek polis, stoic philosophy, and Roman law. See Susan Ford Wiltshire's *Greece, Rome and the Bill of Rights* (Norman and London: University of Oklahoma Press, 1992).

12. See Thomas A. Dooling's discussion of wholeness in the context of jurisprudence, "A Day in Court," *The Parabola Book of Healing* (New York: Continuum Press, 1994).

13. Philip C. Bobbitt, "Barbara Jordan: Constitutional Conscience," 5 Texas J. Women & L. (1996): 171–73.

14. Jordan, "It's More Than a Lifeless Archive." Remarks on Constitution Day Naturalization Ceremony, 17 September 1987, RJT Archives, Houston, Texas.

15. See Earl Conrad, *Jim Crow America* (New York: Sloan & Pierce, 1977); Indus A. Newby, *Jim Crow's Defense: Anti-Negro Thought in America 1900–1930* (Baton Rouge: Louisiana State University Press, 1968); and James H. Jones, *Bad Blood: The Tuskegee Syphilis Experiment* (New York: Free Press, Metropolitan MacMillan Intl., 1993).

16. Theophus H. Smith, *Conjuring Culture: Biblical Formations of Black America* (New York: Oxford University Press, 1994).

17. Jordan, "Testimony House Judiciary Committee," 25 July 1974, Washington, D.C.

18. Berman, *Faith and Order,* 10, quoting John Hiuzinga's *Homo Ludens: A Study of the Play Element in Culture* (Boston: Beacon Press, 1955).

19. Jordan, "Women and the Constitution: : The Challenge," 11 February 1988, Atlanta, Georgia.

20. Hebrews 11:1.

21. See the related discussion of constitutional interpretation in *African Americans and the Living Constitution,* eds. John Hope Franklin and Genna Rae McNeil (Washington and London: Smithsonian Press, 1995).

22. Benjamin Gregg, "The Parameters of Possible Constitutional Interpretation," *Vocabularies of Public Life: Empirical Essays in Symbolic Structure,* ed. Robert Wuthnow (London and New York: Routledge, 1992). See also Stanley Fish, *Is There a Text in this Class?* (Cambridge, Mass: Harvard University Press, 1980), 327; and Sanford Levinson, "Law as Literature," 60 Texas L. Rev. (1982): 373–403.

23. Ibid., 212. Framers of the Constitution adhered to the Lockean doctrine of natural inequality. Jordan notes that the word *equal* and *equality* do not appear in the Constitution. Jordan, "Equality, Liberty, and the Pursuit of Community in America," Texas Committee for the Humanities, University of Texas School of Law, Austin, Texas.

24. Mari J. Matsuda, "When the First Quail Calls: Multiple Consciousness as Jurisprudential Method," 14 Women's Rights Law Reporter (1992): 299.

25. "Response to Mari Matsuda: 1988 Women of Color and the Law Conference at Yale University," 14 Women's Rights Law Reporter (1992): 299.

26. Matsuda, "Multiple Consciousness," 301.

27. Ibid. 299.

28. Du Bois, *The Souls of Black Folk.*

29. White feminists Angela and Sarah Grimké were members of a

wealthy slaveholding family. They publicly claimed a black half-brother. Paula Giddings, *When and Where I Enter: The Impact of Black Women on Race and Sex in America* (New York: Bantam Press, 1984), 43.

30. Matsuda, "Multiple Consciousness," 300.

31. In 1967, President Johnson appointed Thurgood Marshall to succeed Justice Tom Clark. Clark had resigned so that his son could accept the position of attorney general. Prior to his appointment, Marshall had served as solicitor general of the United States, chief counsel of the NAACP, and judge of the Court of Appeals Second Circuit. For further information, see Michael W. Combs, "The Supreme Court, African Americans and Public Policy: Changes, Transformation," *Blacks and the American Political System* (Gainesville: University of Florida Press, 1995), 165.

32. Jordan, 14 July 1987. Hon. Thurgood Marshall, "Remarks given during the 200th Anniversary of the United States Constitution," July 1976, Washington, D.C., Thurgood Marshall Archives, Library of Congress.

33. "The Orison Marden Lecture in Honor of Justice Thurgood Marshall," 47 The Record (1992): 268.

34. Justice Thurgood Marshall, speech at Howard University 18 Nov 1978, in *The Barrister* Jan. 15, 1979, at 1; reprinted in Derrick Bell's *And We Are Not Saved: The Illusive Quest for Racial Justice* 63 (1987).

35. "Constitutional Interpretations," at 234.

36. Jordan, Handwritten speech, n.d., RJT Archives, Houston, Texas.

37. "Constitutional Conscience," 173.

38. Jordan, "Remarks at the Forum Club," 15 July 1991, Houston, Texas.

39. Jordan, "Justice." Remarks before the National Association of Attorneys General Convention, 4 June 1976, San Antonio, Texas. In this speech Jordan discusses the duty of professionals and public officials to translate specialized languages into language understood by the citizenry.

40. Ibid., 2.

41. Ibid., 2.

42. Jordan, "A Celebration of Our African American Legacy," Remarks given at the Thurgood Marshall Legal Society, 17 April 1993, University of Texas, RJT Archives, Austin, Texas.

43. John Rawls, *A Theory of Justice* (Boston: Harvard University Press, 1971).

44. Jordan wrote most but not all of her speeches. However, those that were penned by others consistently reflected her views.

45. Jordan, "Intergenerational Justice," 3.

46. Ibid., 4.

47. 1 Samuel 6:10.

48. Jordan, "We Can't Legislate Happiness," 241, 242.

49. Black Elk, "Black Elk Speaks," as told through John G. Neihardt, *Masterpieces of American Indian Literature,* ed. Willis G. Regier (New York: MJF Books, 1993), 439–621.

Chapter 7: A Beloved, National, and Transcendent Community

1. *To Be Young Gifted and Black* (New York: Samuel French, 1971), 24.

2. Turner, *Blazing the Trail,* 134.

3. Hansberry, *Gifted,* 9.

4. Symbiosis may be defined as a close, prolonged association between two or more different organisms of different species that may, but does not necessarily, benefit each member.

5. de Tocqueville coined the word "individualism" in *Democracy in America,* Garden City, N.Y.: Doubleday, 1975), 98–99.

6. I am making reference to physicist Stephen Hawking's explanation that black holes in space draw matter into a vortex of singularity and extinction.

7. Bounds, *Coming Together/Coming Apart,* 111.

8. Ibid., 120.

9. Ibid., 4.

10. William E. Johnston, Jr., "Finding the Common Good Amidst Democracy's Strange Melancholy: de Tocqueville on Religion and the American's Disgust with Life," *The Journal of Religion* 75 (July 1995): 44–68. The term *culture wars* is taken from James Davison Hunter's book *Culture Wars: The Struggle to Define America* (New York: Basic Books, 1991).

11. Johnston, Finding the Common Good," 44–68.

12. Ibid., 45.

13. Ibid.

14. Jordan, "In Defense of Rights."

15. Jordan, "Setting Priorities," U.S. Commission on Immigration Reform (Washington, D.C.: GPO, 1995), x.

16. Maffesoli, *Tribes,* 16.

17. Ibid.

18. Ibid.

19. Frank G. Kirkpatrick suggests that communities fall into "a trinity of models." They are the atomistic/contractarian, organic/functional, and the mutual/personal models. *Community: A Trinity of Models* (Washington, D.C.: Georgetown University Press, 1986).

20. Perry, "Human Rights," 1032.

21. Jordan, Remarks made at the Television and Radio Advertising

Club, 16 September 1977, Philadelphia, Pennsylvania, RJT Archives, Houston, Texas.

22. Bobbitt, "Constitutional Conscience," 5 Texas J. Women & L. (1996): 172.

23. Baldwin, *To Make the Wounded Whole*, 67.

24. Ibid., 252.

25. Martin Luther King Jr., *Where Do We Go from Here: Chaos or Community?* (Boston: Beacon Press, 1968).

26. When asked about Gandhi, King is reported to have replied "I have read some statements by him" and "I know very little about the man . . . [but] I've always admired him." Stewart Burns, *Daybreak of Freedom: The Montgomery Bus Boycott* (Chapel Hill: University of North Carolina Press, 1997) 21, quoting an interview of Glenn Smiley by David J. Garrow, April 6, 1984, North Hollywood, Calif. King did eventually go to India, where he spent time in the places that inspired Gandhi.

27. Lewis V. Baldwin, *Toward the Beloved Community: Martin Luther King Jr. and South Africa* (Cleveland: Pilgrim Press, 1995).

28. Burns, *Daybreak*, 22.

29. Ibid.

30. Martin Luther King Jr., "The Ethical Demands for Integration" (1962), reprinted in *A Testament of Hope: The Essential Writings of Martin Luther King Jr.*, ed. J. M. Washington (San Francisco: HarperSanFrancisco, 1986), 124.

31. Baldwin, *To Make the Wounded Whole*, 255.

32. The term "world house" is taken from Martin Luther King Jr.'s *Chaos or Community* and is cited in *Testament of Hope*.

33. I am summarizing Baldwin's argument in *To Make the Wounded Whole*.

34. Martin Luther King Jr., Minutes of SCLC Advisory Committee (Nov. 24, 1967), also quoted in D. Garrow's *Bearing the Cross: Martin Luther King Jr., and The Southern Christian Leadership Conference* (New York: William Morrow Press, 1986). See also Anthony E. Cook, "Beyond Critical Legal Studies: The Reconstructive Theology of Dr. Martin Luther King Jr." 103 Harv. L. Rev. (1990): 985, 1040.

35. King, *Chaos or Community*, 189.

36. Ibid., 191.

37. Jordan, "Keynote 1976."

38. Jordan, "Television and Radio," 1.

39. Jordan, "In Pursuit of Community," 3.

40. Ibid.

41. Jordan, "Equality, Liberty and the Pursuit of Community in America," 4, 5, quoting Walter Lippmann's interpretation of Bentham's public philosophy.

42. Ibid., 3, 4.

43. Ibid.

44. Jordan, "Nations in Community," handwritten speech, n.d., RJT Archives, Houston, Texas.

45. David Halberstam, "The Second Coming of Martin Luther King," *Harpers Magazine* 19 (August 1997): 33–53; see also Martin L. King Jr., "A Time To Break Silence," Speech at the Riverside Church, 4 April 1967, *Freedomways* 7: 103–17; also quoted in Garrow, *Bearing the Cross,* 549.

46. George N. Dionisopoulos et al., "Martin Luther King Jr., the American Dream, and Vietnam: A Collision of Rhetorical Trajectories," *Western Journal of Communication* 56 (Spring 1992): 91–107.

47. Jordan, "Intergenerational Justice."

48. Victor Turner, "Liminality and the Performative Genres," *Rite, Drama, Festival, Spectacle: Rehearsals Toward a Theory of Cultural Performance,* ed. John J. MacAloon (Philadelphia: ISHI, 1984).

49. Turner, *The Ritual Process,* 132.

50. Turner, "Morality and Liminality," the Firestone Lecture at the University of Southern California, included in *Blazing the Trail.*

51. Turner, *The Ritual Process.*

52. Ibid.

53. Ibid.

54. Jordan, "Nations in Community," 3.

55. Turner, *Blazing the Trail,* 159.

56. Victor Turner, *Dramas, Fields, and Metaphors: Symbolic Action in Human Society* (Ithaca and London: Cornell University Press, 1974), 56.

57. Hansberry, *Gifted,* 24.

Chapter 8: Conclusion

1. Walter Brueggemann, *Finally Comes the Poet: Daring Speech for Proclamation* (Minneapolis: Fortress Press, 1989), 25.

2. Arthur H. Netherct, "O'Neill's More Stately Mansions," *Educational Theater Journal* (May 1975): 161–69; quoting Mary Mullett's interview with Eugene O'Neill in *The American Magazine* (November 1922). I am grateful for the conversations and research advice of playwright and theater scholar Henry Miller.

3. Ibid.

4. Ibid.

5. Todd Gitlin, *The Twilight of Common Dreams: Why America Is Wracked by Culture Wars* (New York: Henry Holt & Co., 1995), 236.

6. I am summarizing Walter Brueggemann's discussion about the adjudication of human narratives. Unpublished lecture notes, Old Testament Theology, Columbia Theological Seminary, Decatur, Georgia (Fall 1995).

7. Bounds, *Coming Together/Coming Apart,* 4.

8. Jordan, "Dialogue of Barbara Jordan with Maya Angelou," n.d., RJT Archives, Houston, Texas.

9. James Gustafson, *Intersections: Science, Theology, and Ethics* (Cleveland: Pilgrim Press, 1996), 11.

10. Jordan and Hearon, *Barbara Jordan,* 23.

11. Ibid., 24.

Bibliography

Jordan Resources

Bryant, Ira B. *Barbara Charline Jordan: From the Ghetto to the Capitol.* Houston: D. Armstrong Co., 1977.

Jordan, Barbara. Barbara Jordan Archives. Original Speeches, Manuscripts, Papers, and Letters. Robert J. Terry Library, Texas Southern University, Houston, Texas.

Jordan, Barbara, and Shelby Hearon. *Barbara Jordan: A Self-Portrait.* New York: Doubleday & Co., Inc., 1979.

Jordan, Barbara, and Elspeth D. Rostow, eds. *The Great Society: A Twenty-Year Critique.* Austin: University of Texas Press, 1986.

Books

Alexander, Bobby C. *Victor Turner Revisited: Ritual as Social Change.* Atlanta: Scholars Press, 1991.

Anderson, Victor. *Beyond Ontological Blackness: An Essay on African American Religious and Cultural Criticism.* New York: Continuum Press, 1995.

Andrews, James R. *The Practice of Rhetorical Criticism.* New York: Longman Press, 1990.

Audi, Robert, and Nicholas Wolterstorff. *Religion in the Public Square: The Place of Religious Convictions in Political Debate.* New York: Rowman & Littlefield Publishers, 1997.

Baldwin, James. *Just Above My Head.* New York: The Dial Press, 1979.

———. *The Price of the Ticket: Collected Nonfiction 1948–1985.* New York: St. Martin's/Marek, 1985.

Baldwin, Lewis V. *To Make the Wounded Whole.* Minneapolis: Fortress Press, 1992.

———. *There is a Balm in Gilead: The Cultural Roots of Martin Luther King Jr.* Minneapolis: Fortress Press, 1991.

———. *Toward the Beloved Community: Martin Luther King Jr. in South Africa.* Cleveland: Pilgrim Press, 1995.

Bellah, Robert, et al. *Habits of the Heart: Individualism and Commitment in American Life.* Berkeley: University of California Press, 1985.

Berman, Harold J. *Faith and Order: The Reconciliation of Law and Religion.* Atlanta: Scholars Press, 1993.

Bounds, Elizabeth M. *Coming Together/Coming Apart: Religion, Community, and Modernity.* New York and London: Routledge, 1997.

Brissett, Dennis, and Charles Edgley, eds. *Life as Theatre.* 2d ed. New York: Aldine de Gruyter, 1990.

Brock, Bernard L., and Robert L. Scott, et al. *Methods of Rhetorical Criticism: A Twentieth-Century Perspective.* Detroit: Wayne State University Press, 1989.

Burke, Kenneth. *Language as Symbolic Action: Essays on Life, Literature, and Method.* Berkeley: University of California Press, 1966.

———. *A Rhetoric of Motives.* New York: Prentice-Hall, 1945.

———. *The Philosophy of Literary Form.* New York: Random House, 1957.

———. *Rhetoric of Religion: Studies in Logology.* Berkeley: University of California Press, 1969.

Cady, Linell E. *Religion, Theology, and American Public Life.* Albany: State University of New York Press, 1993.

Care, Norman S. *On Sharing Fate.* Philadelphia: Temple University Press, 1987.

Casanova, José. *Public Religions in the Modern World.* Chicago: University of Chicago Press, 1994.

Caudill, David, and Steven Gold. *Radical Philosophy of Law: Contemporary Challenges to Mainstream Legal Theory and Practice.* Atlantic Highlands, N.J.: Humanities Press, 1995.

Cohen, Morris R. *Reason and Law: Studies in Juristic Philosophy.* Glencoe, Ill.: Free Press, 1950.

Cotterrell, Roger. *Law's Community: Legal Theory in Sociological Perspective.* New York: Oxford University Press, 1995.

Denton, Robert E., ed. *Ethical Dimensions of Political Communication.* New York: Praeger Press, 1991.

Du Bois, W. E. B. *The Souls of Black Folk.* New York: NAL Penguin, 1969.

Dyson, Michael E. *Making Malcolm: The Myth and Meaning of Malcolm X.* New York and Oxford: Oxford University Press, 1995.

Erdman, Harley. *Staging the Jew: The Performance of An American Ethnicity 1860–1920.* New Brunswick, N.J.: Rutgers University Press, 1997.

Early, Gerald, ed. *Lure and Loathing: Essays on Race, Identity, and the Ambivalence of Assimilation.* New York: Penguin Press, 1993.

Elliot, Jeffrey M. *Black Voices in American Politics.* San Diego, Calif.: Harcourt Brace Jovanovich Publishers, 1986.

Epps, Archie, ed. *Malcolm X: Speeches at Harvard.* New York: Paragon House, 1991.

Firth, Raymond. *Religion: A Humanist Interpretation.* New York and London: Routledge, 1996.

Gadamer, Hans-Georg. *Truth and Method.* 2d ed. New York: Continuum Press, 1994.

Gordon, Avery F., and Christopher Newfield, eds. *Mapping Multiculturalism.* Minneapolis: University of Minnesota Press, 1996.

Gustafson, James M. *Intersections: Science, Theology, and Ethics.* Cleveland: Pilgrim Press, 1996.

Guy-Sheftall, Beverly. *Words of Fire: An Anthology of African-American Feminist Thought.* New York: The New Press, 1995.

Farrell, James J. *The Spirit of the Sixties: The Making of Postwar Radicalism.* New York: Routledge, 1997.

Halprin, Sara. *Look at My Ugly Face: Myths and Musings on Beauty and Other Perilous Obsessions with Women's Appearance.* New York: Viking Press, 1995.

Han, Edwin L, ed. *The Philosophy of Hans-Georg Gadamer.* The Library of Living Philosophers. Vol. 24. Chicago: Open Court, 1997.

Handler, Joel F. *Law and the Search for Community.* Philadelphia: University of Pennsylvania Press, 1990.

Hare, Paul A., and Herbert H. Blumberg. *Dramaturgical Analysis of Social Interaction.* New York: Praeger Press, 1988.

Harrod, Howard L. *The Human Center: Moral Agency in the Social World.* Philadelphia: Fortress Press, 1981.

Haskins, James. *Barbara Jordan.* New York: The Dial Press, 1977.

Heinzelman, Susan, and Zipporah Wiseman. *Representing Women: Law, Literature, and Feminism.* Durham, N.C.: Duke University Press, 1994.

Heschel, Abraham Joshua. *I Asked for Wonder: A Spiritual Anthology.* New York: Crossroad, 1991.

hooks, bell. *Black Looks: Race and Representation.* Boston: South End Press, 1992.

———. *Yearning: Race, Gender and Cultural Politics.* Boston: South End Press, 1990.

Horwitz, Morton J. *The Transformation of American Law 1870–1960: The Crisis of Legal Orthodoxy.* New York: Oxford University Press, 1992.

Hunt, Alan. *Explorations in Law and Society: Towards a Constitutive Theory of Law.* New York: Routledge, 1993.

James, Stanlie M., and Abema P. A. Busia. *Theorizing Black Feminisms: The Visionary Pragmatism of Black Women.* London: Routledge, 1993.

Jewell, Sue K. *From Mammy to Miss America and Beyond: Cultural Images and the Shaping of U.S. Social Policy.* London and New York: Routledge, 1993.

Johnson, Peter. *Politics, Innocence, and the Limits of Goodness.* New York and London: Routledge, 1988.

King Jr., Martin L. *Where Do We Go From Here?: Chaos or Community.* Boston: Beacon Press, 1968.

Lewis, David L. *W. E. B. Du Bois: Biography of a Race.* New York: Henry Holt & Co., 1993.

Lorde, Audre. *The Black Unicorn: Poems by Audre Lorde.* New York: W. W. Norton & Co., 1978.

————. *Sister Outsider: Essays and Speeches by Audre Lorde.* Trumansburg, N.Y.: The Crossing Press, 1984.

Lundin, Roger. *Disciplining Hermeneutics: Interpretation in Christian Perspective.* Grand Rapids, Mich.: Wm. B. Eerdmans, 1997.

Lunsford, Andrea A. *Reclaiming Rhetorica: Women in the Rhetorical Tradition.* Pittsburgh: University of Pittsburgh Press, 1995.

Maffesoli, Michel. *The Time of the Tribes: The Decline of Individualism in Mass Society.* Translated by Don Smith. London: Sage Publications, 1996.

McNeil, Genna Rae, and John Hope Franklin. *African Americans and the Living Constitution.* Washington and London: Smithsonian Institution Press, 1995.

Molnar, Thomas. *Twin Powers: Politics and the Sacred.* Grand Rapids, Mich.: Wm. B. Eerdmans, 1988.

Mullen, Edward J. *Critical Essays on Langston Hughes.* Boston: G. K. Hall & Co., 1986.

Olafson, Frederick A. *Society, Law, and Morality: Readings in Social Philosophy from Classical and Contemporary Sources.* Englewood Cliffs, N.J.: Prentice-Hall, 1961.

Page, Clarence. *Showing My Color: Impolite Essays on Race and Identity.* New York: HarperCollins Publishers, 1996.

Raskin, Marcus G. *The Common Good: Its Politics, Policies, and Philosophy.* New York and London: Routledge, 1986.

Selznick, Philip. *The Moral Commonwealth: Social Theory and the Promise of Community.* Berkeley: University of California Press, 1992.

Shanks, Andrew. *Civil Society, Civil Religion.* Oxford: Blackwell Press, 1995.

Silverman, Hugh J. *Writing the Politics of Difference.* New York; University of New York Press, 1991.

Smith, Patricia. *Feminist Jurisprudence.* New York: Oxford University Press, 1993.

Standley, Fred L., and Louis H. Pratt, eds. *Conversations with James Baldwin.* Jackson: University Press of Mississippi, 1989.

Tierney, Brian. *The Idea of Natural Rights: Studies on Natural Rights, Natural Law, and Church Law 1150–1625.* Atlanta: Scholars Press, 1997.

Torrance, Robert M. *The Spiritual Quest: Transcendence in Myth, Religion, and Science.* Berkeley: University of California Press, 1994.

Turner, Victor. *Blazing the Trail: Way Marks in the Exploration of Symbols.* Edited by Edith Turner. Tucson: University of Arizona Press, 1992.

———. *Dramas, Fields, and Metaphors: Symbolic Action in Human Society.* Ithaca and London: Cornell University Press, 1974.

———. *The Ritual Process: Structure and Anti-Structure.* Chicago: University of Chicago Press, 1969.

Walker, Robbie Jean, ed. *The Rhetoric of Struggle: Public Address by African American Women.* New York: Garland Publishing, 1992.

Washington, James M., ed. *A Testament of Hope: The Essential Writings and Speeches of Martin Luther King Jr.* San Francisco: Harper & Row, 1986.

Wetherell, Margaret, and Jonathan Potter. *Mapping the Language of Racism.* New York: Columbia University Press, 1992.

Wiltshire, Susan Ford. *Greece, Rome and the Bill of Rights.* Norman and London: University of Oklahoma Press, 1992.

Young, Iris M. *Throwing Like a Girl and Other Essays in Feminist Philosophy and Social Theory.* Indianapolis: Indiana University Press, 1990.

Journals and Legal Citations

Baker-Kelly, Beverly. *United States Immigration: A Wake Up Call.* 37 Howard L.J. (1994): 283–304.

Brown-Scott, Wendy. *Justice Thurgood Marshall and the Integrative Ideal.* 26 Ariz. St. L. (Summer 1994): 535–60.

Cook, Anthony E. *Beyond Critical Legal Studies: The Reconstructive Theology of Dr. Martin Luther King Jr.* 103 Harv. L. Rev. (1994): 985–1044.

Culp, Jerome. *Color-Blind Remedies and the Inter-sectionality of Oppression: Policy Arguments Masquerading as Moral Claims.* 69 N.Y.U. L. Rev. (1994): 162–92.

Gronbeck, Bruce E. "Dramaturgical Theory and Criticism: The State of the Art (or Science?)." *The Western Journal of Speech Communication* 44 (Fall 1980): 315–30.

Johnston, William E. "Finding the Common Good Amidst Democracy's Strange Melancholy: Tocqueville on Religion and the American's 'Disgust with Life.'" *The Journal of Religion* 75 (July 1995): 44–68.

Lipkin, Robert J. *Kibitzers, Fuzzies, and Apes Without Tails: Pragmatism and the Art of Conversation in Legal Theory.* 66 Tulane L. Rev. (1991): 69–139.

Matsuda, Mari J. *Pragmatism Modified and the False Consciousness Problem.* 63 So. Calif. L. Rev. (1990): 1763–81.

———. *When the First Quail Calls: Multiple Consciousness as Jurisprudential Method.* 14 Women's Rights Law Reporter (1992): 299–301.

Smith, Arthur L. "Markings of an African Concept of Rhetoric." *Today's Speech* 19 (1971): 13–17.

———. "Socio-historical Perspectives of Black Oratory." *Quarterly Journal of Speech* 56 (1970): 249–69.

West, Cornel. *The Limits of NeoPragmatism.* 63 So. Calif. L. Rev. (1990): 1747–51.

Index

African Americans. *See* black
church; black women
American Indians, 64, 104–5
Americanization of immigrants,
67–69, 141n68
Anderson, Victor, 45, 132n10
Angelou, Maya, 126
assimilation, 67–69, 134n39,
141n68

Baldwin, James, 34–36, 43, 69, 84,
136n18
Baldwin, Lewis V., 114
Bell, Daniel, 110–11
Bellah, Robert, 65
beloved community, 8, 110, 113–
15, 118–19, 121
Bentham, Jeremy, 117
Berman, Harold J., 9, 96
Black, Justice Hugo, 130n10
black church, role of, 21, 71,
83–87, 134n40, 135n10
Black Elk (Native American
spiritualist), 104–5
black women, roles of, 21, 83–84,
134n40, 135n10
Bobbitt, Philip, 94, 101, 113
Boston University Law School, vii,
19, 71
Bounds, Elizabeth M., 110, 125
Brueggemann, Walter, 124
Bryant, Ira, 16
Buber, Martin, 121
Burke, Kenneth, 8–9, 47, 127,
131nn14–16, 18, 133n30,
140n65
Burns, Stewart, 114
Bush, George H. W., 17, 39

Casanova, José, 79
Cherokee Indians, 64

church, role in public life, 7,
10, 48–49, 71–87, 94–101,
130n10
civil rights movement, 29–37, 95,
113, 119, 135, 136n17
Clark, Justice Tom, 146n31
Clinton, William Jefferson, 46,
57–59
color politics, 13–15. *See also*
racism
common good
envisioning, 6, 33, 51–56,
59–62, 126
government and, 46, 50–53,
56–57, 101–3, 125n11
pluralism and, 60, 62–69
public theology and, 60, 87–90,
114
See also community
common values, 51–56, 61, 68. *See
also* mutuality
communitas, 8, 110, 120–21, 126,
131n19
community
beloved, 8, 110, 113–15, 118–
19, 121
concepts of, 3–7, 104, 109–17,
147n19
national community, 4–5, 61,
92, 116–19, 125–26
public discourse and, 30, 51–52,
94–95, 110–11, 117, 123
transcendent community, 79,
111, 119–21
See also common values; communitas; government, purpose
of
Cone, James, 72
consciousness, multiple, 97–99,
103. *See also* pluralism

157